RELENTLESS

9/98

ALSO BY JOHNY K. JOHANSSON
Global Marketing

ALSO BY IKUJIRO NONAKA
The Knowledge-Creating Company (with Hirotaka Takeuchi)
Strategic vs. Evolutionary Management (with Tadao Kagono et al.)

RELENTLESS

 ## THE JAPANESE WAY OF MARKETING

*Johny K. Johansson and
Ikujiro Nonaka*

HarperBusiness

A Division of HarperCollinsPublishers

Sc1

A hardcover edition of this book was published in 1996 by HarperBusiness, a division of HarperCollins Publishers.

HarperCollins books may be purchased for educational, business, or sales promotional use. For information please write: Special Markets Department, HarperCollins Publishers, Inc., 10 East 53rd Street, New York, NY 10022.

First paperback edition published 1997.

Designed by Irving Perkins Associates

The Library of Congress has catalogued the hardcover edition as follows:

Johansson, Johny K.
    Relentless : the Japanese way of marketing / Johny K. Johansson. — 1st ed.
      198 p. 25 cm.
    Includes bibliographic references and index.
    ISBN 0-88730-805-8
    1. Marketing—Japan. 2. Export marketing. I. Nonaka, Ikujiro. II. Title.
  HF5415.12.J3 J63   1996

                                                96-170930

ISBN 0-88730-860-0 (pbk.)

97 98 99 00 01 ❖/RRD 10 9 8 7 6 5 4 3 2 1

For Franco Nicosia, our mentor at Berkeley

CONTENTS

PREFACE

Today, market-based transactions are everywhere. How good a job you can land and hold depends on what the market value of your skills are, not on what you happen to think your contribution is. Old loyalties go by the wayside as reengineering makes your training obsolete. As a consumer, you are supposed to make informed decisions not only about the usual products and services but about health insurance, telephone carriers, retirement plans, and on-line services. And the moment you have made your decision, new alternatives spring up claiming better performance, lower price, and new features. While free markets may be good for us as consumers, they require a lot of confusing choices to be made. For companies hoping to compete, the stress is even higher, as new competitors and new products arrive daily. Not surprisingly, many companies have resorted to unflinching cost cutting, including layoffs, to stay competitive. It's a dog-eat-dog kind of world.

This book is basically about good marketing practice. It demonstrates the philosophy involved in a true customer orientation and what it takes to earn and justify customer allegiance. It shows how incumbent market leaders can be successfully challenged and what it takes to stay competitive over the long run. But it also suggests that there is a better solution to company survival than laying off people. It demonstrates how the front-line personnel and the workers can become the company's distinguishing resource, not by working harder but by working differently. And destroying this resource by layoffs is equivalent to shooting oneself in the foot.

The logic is very simple. Customer satisfaction does not come from managers. It comes from superior products and services and from the attitude and skills of the people who deal directly with the customers. Managers don't make the products—workers do. Managers don't talk to customers—service people do.

Actually, Japanese managers do talk to customers. The Japanese have been extraordinarily successful in creating high customer satisfaction. They are excellent at manufacturing products and at providing service. In manufacturing and after-sales service, Western companies have learned a lot from the Japanese. As we intend to show, the Japanese are also good marketers—but with a recipe for success that is very different from the standard Western fare. In Japanese companies, managers believe in their employees. In Japanese companies, managers support the front-line people. In Japanese companies, laying off workers means that the manager, not the worker, failed.

This book is about the Japanese way of marketing. It deals with Japanese companies' marketing practices, the way they design market-based products, how they do market research, the way they set prices, the way they advertise, and the way they construct their channels of distribution. But, equally important, it deals with the way they think about themselves as marketers, what the seller's and buyer's roles are, what *customer satisfaction* means, what a long-term relationship involves, and what is important in personal selling. It is in their philosophy about marketing that the Japanese differ most markedly from the West, and it is this philosophy that makes it so simple for them to develop effective marketing practices. Adopting the best Japanese practices without at the same time rethinking the role of the marketer and the customer means that the company only gets half of the benefits. Adopting a new philosophy might be harder for Western companies than adopting new practices—changing how one thinks might be harder than changing what one does—but without it, the edge might still be with the Japanese.

This book combines two perspectives on Japanese marketing philosophy and practice. It draws on in-depth knowledge of the Japanese organizations' strategies and tactics—the field of inquiry that has occupied Ikujiro for the better part of the last twenty-five years. It combines this with the Western perspective on Japanese practices, an area of research for Johny for the last fifteen years. The book draws not only on material from the Japanese companies but also on information from their Western competitors in Japan and elsewhere. We think the dual perspective sheds additional light on what is significant about the observed practices, because it is often difficult for insiders to recognize what outsiders find most new and striking. Just as the Japanese seem to have discovered things about Western consumers that were not noticed by Western marketers, there are things about the Japanese marketers' way of doing marketing that go unnoticed by them because they are so natural. The book aims to bring out these seemingly self-evident but powerful principles of marketing for all of us to learn from.

ACKNOWLEDGMENTS

We owe a first debt of gratitude to all the Japanese managers who have spent time with us over the past ten years or so as the ideas in this book were formed. Much of the material presented is distilled from interviews and data collected as we spent time with managers and their teams in executive teaching or for various research and consulting projects. Although some of them are quoted directly in the book, many others have also contributed.

We have interviewed managers in many Japanese companies, and although it is not possible to name them all, we want to mention some who have been particularly influential. Mitsuya Goto, formerly of Nissan; Osamu Iida, Saburo Kobayashi, and Norimoto Otsuka of Honda; Akira Toriyama at Mazda; and Shigero Handa at Toyota were some of the key informants on the auto industry. Kozo Ohsone at Sony, Shoji Hiroe at Toshiba, Minoru Sakamoto at Mitsubishi Electric, and Toshihiro Minami at Hitachi all provided useful information on the electronics industry. An early influence was Masahiko Kuninaga at Matsushita, who, tragically, was killed in the 1985 crash of a JAL 747 near Mount Fuji. Kiyofumi Matsumoto at Canon, Ned Moro at Minolta, Tsuyoshi Mano at Kyocera, Ted Hirose of Shin-Nippon Wex, Hiroshi Ohnishi of Core Company in Osaka, Masumi Natsuzaka at Kao, Casey Shimamoto at Daiwa Securities, and Hiroe Suzuki of Dentsu also provided new information and fresh perspectives on many issues in their respective industries. Hideo Shimoda at Jetro helped arrange many company interviews over the years.

We have also benefited from talking to managers in many Western companies with ties to Japan, including Hideo Hohgi of BMW Japan, Hans-Olov Olsson and Rune Lundberg at Volvo Japan, Richard Laube at P&G Japan, James Hubbert at Disney Japan, Jan Segerfeldt in Stockholm, and Ron Hosogi of Microsoft. Jack Huddleston and his seminar speakers from Japan at the University of Washington, Mitchell Reed at Grey Daiko, and Karl-Herman Gistren at Gadelius K.K. in Tokyo were key sources for information on the intense competition inside Japan faced by Western companies.

Overseas, we have learned much from interviews with the managers at

Japanese subsidiaries in North America as well as Europe. Chris Wada of Sony America; Osamu Iida of Honda North America; Andre Meganck of Honda in Europe; Masashi Kuga of Jergens Company, a subsidiary of Kao; and Hiroyuki Tezuka of NKK's Washington office were particularly informative.

Needless to say, we have also gained a lot from interactions with our peers at academic institutions. In Japan, they include Tadao Kagono at Kobe, Hirotaka Takeuchi at Hitotsubashi, Akihiro Okumura and Mitsuo Wada at Keio Business School, and Masaaki Hirano at Waseda. Jerry Sullivan at the University of Washington in Seattle, Tom Roehl at the University of Illinois, Vlad Pucik at Cornell, Phil Kotler at Northwestern, and George Yip at UCLA have influenced our thinking to a great extent. So have Kiyonori Sakakibara at the London Business School and Gunnar Hedlund at the Stockholm School of Economics.

To all these people, many not mentioned here, and many not necessarily agreeing with our analysis and conclusions, our thanks. We also want to thank our editor at HarperBusiness, Kirsten Sandberg, whose encouragement and active voice helped crystallize our ideas and make many sentences less "obscurely academic." Jennifer Barker was an excellent and patient typist, always willing to work against tight deadlines—thank you. And we want to apologize to our respective families. While authors often can enjoy the writing of a book—as we did—for the families, it is basically a painful process. We hope it was worth it.

INTRODUCTION

WHY BOTHER ABOUT JAPAN NOW?

Why should anybody bother about the Japanese companies today after all the troubles in Japan? The reason is simple. The Japanese companies are coming back. They are still very competitive—and they still do things differently from their Western competitors.

Paradox: After three to four years of mainly negative news out of Japan, Japanese companies are still major players in world markets.

Item: Toyota's second-wave assault on the U.S. market, opening a truck plant in Indiana, leads *Business Week* (December 18) to issue a warning: "Watch out, Detroit. I think they were just lying low."

Item: Sony reins in free-spending top manager Michael Schulhof, increasing Tokyo control—but also increasing expansion into the "digital dream kid" role new CEO Nobuyuki Idei envisions.

Item: While Ford's restyled Taurus is no success—at least, not yet—and Taurus is no longer the bestselling car in America, the new Honda Accord is, and the new Honda Civic is the 1996 car of the year.

What is happening seems like the second coming of the Japanese. It is a paradox. While the American economy has been doing well, the Japanese economy has not. But profitable American companies lay off people in large restructuring moves, focusing on financial asset leveraging and treating labor as exchangeable parts. European business, despite the boon of integration, fails to make a dent in the level of unemployment, which at 10-plus percent is at levels unheard of since World War II. Japanese unemployment, despite dire circumstances, is still less than 5 percent, as companies resist wholesale layoffs. The Japanese actions seem designed to induce the "British malaise," a recipe for making industry uncompetitive, firms of low productivity, and a sick economy.

Apparently not, as Japanese companies maintain momentum in world markets and threaten to grab even larger market share in mature industries: autos, consumer and industrial electronics, cameras, and steel. Japanese quality is still a world-class standard-setter, and customer satisfaction scores are still higher than before. They are also still ahead of most Western products, however vastly improved those have been under the influence of the first wave of the Japanese "invasion."

NEW MARKETING THINKING IN THE WEST

The recent crop of bestsellers on marketing practices in the West exhort managers to follow principles that are typical of Japanese practices.

Item: Treacy and Wiersema in the 1995 bestseller *The Discipline of Market Leaders* explain what product leadership demands:

> What so distinguishes product leadership firms from most other companies today is that product leaders don't slavishly follow the voice of the customer. The customer can't define for them the next breakthrough product. Market researchers can't define it, either. Although product leaders like Intel stay close to the market, they listen to the astute comments of the customers only to hone their own judgment of the future. Customers can help them get the details right [p. 104].

In the chapters on customer satisfaction (chapter 2) and marketing research (chapter 3), we explain how the Japanese for years have been reading between the lines of customer responses, and also show what it takes to do it.

Item: Later in their book, Treacy and Wiersema argue for the need to make more than cosmetic changes:

> Market leaders place their leadership in jeopardy when they exploit value at the expense of innovation. Pepsi, for some reason, believes that dating its soda cans will generate more consumer demand, and Coke believes that reintroducing in plastic the corset-shaped bottle that helped make it famous will rejuvenate the brand. Meanwhile, Snapple and other aspiring leaders are making sharp inroads in the soft drink market. Their "secret": they're doing real product innovation instead of just tinkering with their package design [p. 197].

In the chapter entitled "Making That Product," we show how the Japanese have managed to be customer-oriented by being product-oriented, and how this means that engineers and designers have to be marketers as well.

Item: The need for lateral communication and integration between production and marketing is emphasized by Moore in his insightful 1995 book on marketing in the Silicon Valley, *Inside the Tornado*:

Marketing, in the engineering universe, is that place where the laws of utility are suspended. They are of two minds about this. On the one hand, if painting the product red sells more product, by all means paint it red. On the other hand, since there is no rational cause operating here, you cannot trust marketing, as anyone can see for themselves, since sometimes when they paint it red, it does not sell more. So marketing is essentially voodoo. It is for flakes. It is not a real discipline. It is a con job.

And that is when engineering is being nice. . . . in fact it represents a life-threatening disability when it comes to Main Street success. Because on Main Street continued high profit margin can only come from end users sponsoring our product over the low-cost clone, and the only thing that will get them to do that is to deliver them subjective experiences of the product that fulfills their needs. That means engineering must learn to authentically empower marketing [pp. 113–114].

The Japanese have long considered marketing a business for everyone in the company, not a professional pursuit of some specialists, and Japanese engineers, designers, and top managers have a tradition of participating in sales efforts, marketing research, and service calls. But this requires a redefinition of what leadership is about, and marketers have to change their self-perceptions and how they define who is a customer. The first chapter of the book deals with this issue of professional versus amateur marketers.

Item: The Sam Walton success story has supplied grist for several new marketing books. One comes from Guy Kawasaki, a former marketer in the Macintosh Division of Apple, whose entertaining *How to Drive Your Competition Crazy* became a best-seller in 1995. Walton's story, of course, fits well with the idea of not treating marketing as a professional specialty, our thrust in chapter 1. Kawasaki reports on Walton's trips to various competitors' stores to see firsthand what they were doing, and concludes:

Competitive research starts at the top. It isn't something to delegate to underlings, the marketing department, or consultants. . . . The best researcher is often the person who is going to use the information to make decisions. This person can see nuances and traps that escape others. . . . Competitive research isn't hard and necessarily expensive. For many organizations, it just means getting out of your chair, getting in a car or plane, and seeing what the competition is doing [p. 41].

The Japanese, and this book, offer several examples of this "hands-on" research style, and of how the learning can be shared throughout the organization.

Item: The Walton story also offers good examples of competitive imitation. Again Guy Kawasaki:

Don't be proud. Walton readily admits copying Kmart as he built up Wal-Mart. He admits he copied Price Club when he started Sam's Club. If you see a good idea, adapt it to your own needs but also be aware that part of being a good thief is knowing what to steal [p. 42].

Targeting competitors, as we call it in chapter 5, has long been a mainstay of Japanese marketing. It tends to destroy what has come to be called "first-mover advantages," as another recent marketing trade book, *Managing Imitation Strategies*, by Steven Schnaars, also points out. In our book we show how the practices of reverse engineering and benchmarking are examples of imitative practices that come naturally only after uniqueness and ego-driven we-are-special obstacles have been cleared.

Item: Hamel and Prahalad's 1994 book, *Competing for the Future*, *Business Week*'s "Best Management Book of the Year," touches on marketing only intermittently. Nevertheless, the advice to practice "expeditionary marketing" is drawn directly from the Japanese way:

Expeditionary marketing does not imply launching products that are manifestly unready or inappropriate to the needs of potential customers. Expeditionary marketing honors the quality maxim, "conformance to customer requirement," but recognizes that customer requirements in emerging markets can only be partially understood. There is much that cannot be known about customer needs, the suitability of particular technologies, and viable price-performance combinations in the absence of direct market experimentation. But expeditionary marketing is not a blind leap of faith; each product iteration should embody all that is currently possible to know about customer needs and desires [pp. 241–242].

Hamel and Prahalad draw on Japanese examples (Toshiba laptops, Japanese autos) to illustrate the concept of expeditionary marketing. We think practicing expeditionary marketing is a tough challenge for most marketers, even the Japanese, since the concept calls for perfection and speed, flexibility and expertise, all at the same time. But in our book (chapters 4 and 5) we show how these seeming contradictions have been erased by Japanese companies.

We do not want to suggest that what these new books advocate is all based on the Japanese way with marketing—they are not. Nor do we want to suggest that this book only concerns Japanese practices with clear counterparts in the West—it does not. But we want to suggest that (1) many of the lessons one can learn from these recent books have already been practiced by the Japanese, and (2) to fully derive the benefits from the adoption of these practices, Western marketers need to understand the change in mindset required, about customers and competitors—and about the marketers themselves.

This book shows how the Japanese way with marketing fits these patterns perfectly. But the point of the book is not simply that. The main message is that marketers need to change their thinking to maximize the benefits of the Japanese way. Our suggestions for marketers go along with much of the recent professional management literature—only we attempt to get under the surface of the obvious practices and approaches proposed for Western managers and already employed by the Japanese.

The fact is that Western adoption of Japanese practices has been less effective than it should be. Many Western companies have adopted the Japanese way only reluctantly—not being sure it will work here. For them it seems mainly to involve a lot of work (it does), and "it won't work here" (it will—with a changed mindset). Furthermore, the work involved will lessen once the thinking behind Japanese practices is understood. Western thinking puts up obstacles that only increase the work involved in changing to better practices. The problem with the Japanese way is in the minds of the Western people.

ANTICIPATING THE ARGUMENT

What is so different about the Japanese way with marketing?

The book rejects three dualisms as starting points in the mind-set transition (Western emphasis on dualism is a matter of concern to Japanese managers, who think they mainly create false contradictions).

- Get rid of the dualism involved in *making* and *selling*. This simple split is misleading also to Mintzberg in his 1994 book, *The Rise and Fall of Strategic Planning,* because it creates a gap between what you make and what you sell.
- Get rid of the dualism between *engineers* and *marketers*. Even engineers need to reach out and touch the customer/consumer. Moore, in his book *Inside the Tornado,* is good on the difficulty engineers have in handling marketing questions.
- Get rid of the dualism between *professionals* and *amateurs*. Professionals are all too often defined by what they don't do ("I don't do marketing research")—suicidal in the new economy.

The Japanese want to get rid of these opposites to (1) avoid barriers to lateral communication inside the corporation between marketing and design/manufacturing, (2) force engineers to deal with customers, and (3) teach that products are for enabling people to live, not constraining them.

- The recipe for success in consumer durables has been for the Japanese to probe more deeply into consumers' desires, and to provide intrinsic product improvement (quality, reliability), coupled with augmenting factors such as service, where Western companies have focused (when competing at all).
- The Japanese advantage is that they have turned mature and staid markets into exciting new product arenas, waking up customers and competitors alike.
- Their way of effecting this change has shifted the rules of the competitive game toward their advantages in implementation and execution.

The Japanese have:

- Increased the speed of new product introductions.
- Offered intrinsic improvements in mature products, not only cosmetic changes or extrinsic add-ons.
- Been able to read between the lines and learn how to get under the skin of the customers in mature markets.
- Properly trained and paid for the important role of the middlemen, their "first" customers.
- Stayed very close to their customers from the beginning.

The end result has been to create a new type of competitive game in mature markets, still fighting for market share, but with a much more pampered and demanding consumer, with both intrinsic and extrinsic demands. The consequent emphasis on customer satisfaction has been a bonanza to Japanese while Western people are still very ego-driven when dealing with the customer.

THE PARTS

The way the Japanese marketers think about themselves and their customers is the subject of the first three chapters. This part we call "Breaking the Mold," since it involves reconceptualizing the standard way of thinking. The professionalism inculcated by Western individualism (chapter 1) creates an invisible barrier when it comes to marketing, since it leads to internal organizational barriers that go against the necessary everything-is-marketing notion. The same problem occurs when approaching the customer (chapter 2), since the problem solved is usually that of the seller, not the buyer. The marketer's ego stands in the way of true customer service, and the best intentions are ruined by a lack of intuitive understanding of the proper roles of buyers and sellers. Chapter 3 elaborates on the fact that even engineers have to approach customers, and learn from them, a concept very common in today's management literature in the West, especially among high-tech companies.

In the second part of the book, two chapters deal with what we call "Intuitive Strategists." Chapter 4 treats the incrementalism for which the Japanese are famous, and shows how this becomes a natural, intuitive, and, not the least, comfortable approach to strategy for amateurs. It also explains how speed and flexibility—execution of strategy—create their own competitive dynamics. It leads into a chapter on targeting competitors (chapter 5) that shows how the Japanese continually upend the marketplace, by taking no prisoners, by churning and driving the competition crazy, in Guy Kawasaki's apt phrase.

The third part of the book, "Getting It Done," deals with other marketing actions. Chapter 6 shows how new products and product-line questions are at the heart of the Japanese marketing mix, and shows how the products get made. The Japanese mold breaking and strong intuition lead to different ways of approaching pricing and advertising questions (chapter 7) and to differences in the management of distribution channels (chapter 8).

The last chapter (chapter 9) puts it all together and shows why the Japanese have been able to conquer new markets in the West—cartoons, toys, popular arts—in areas where the home market does not seem to give them an advantage. This chapter also gets into the downside of the Japanese approach, showing that the narrow focus on execution and the here-and-now can lead them astray. It is in fact the avoidance of such mistakes that turns out to be the advantage of the Western way—and at the end we clarify under what circumstances the Japanese way is not so useful—and, by implication, where it has most power.

BREAKING THE MOLD

PART I

BREAKING THE MOLD

I

THE JAPANESE MARKETERS

Many customers are surprised to learn that marketing is a technical business function and an academic discipline. Like the engineers in Silicon Valley described by Geoffrey Moore in *Inside the Tornado*, they might think of marketing as salesmanship or voodoo, with the associated negative connotations. But in the modern corporation in the West (by which we basically mean Western Europe and North America) marketing strategies and plans can be as elaborate and well-researched as the offensive game plan for a team in the Super Bowl. For example, before Buick introduced its upscale sports car the Reatta in 1988, the GM division, according to one count, had conducted seventeen different studies between 1981 and 1987 to help identify the most effective positioning against competing makes.[1] Despite this effort, the positioning remained uncertain, and the last two studies just before the planned launch split between a "luxury" position and a "sports car" position. Reatta was positioned as a "luxury car for two" and had some initial success until the Mazda Miata from Japan was introduced and lowered the price/value ratio for sporty cars.

As marketing becomes more important and global competition affects their companies, some managers reluctantly recognize that, to do their jobs, they need to learn more about marketing. When they open up a standard text of marketing management, they are impressed by the bulk of material and awed by its complexity. Marketing seems to be a science, and serious marketing is a game for professionals only. Or is it?

THE "SCIENCE" OF MARKETING

The fact is that many nonprofessional marketers with strong intuition—
Mary Kay's cosmetics, the Body Shop, Benetton—have done very well,
while many professional marketers—Coca Cola with its New Coke, Ford
with its new Edsel and new Taurus, and Reebok with its "Be yourself"
campaign—have stumbled. While some professional campaigns are very
impressive, the next effort by the same agency easily falls flat. Thus with
IBM's PC (a successful launch with the DOS operating system) and OS/2
(its second operating system, a failure), with Disney in Japan (very successful) and Disney in Europe (Euro-Disney has been having its share of
setbacks), with Miller's Lite (a success) and Miller's High Life (with weak
sales, positioned against Budweiser), and with Procter & Gamble's
Pampers (global leader in disposable diapers) and Citrus Hill (P&G's discontinued orange juice).

THE PROFESSIONAL NONPROFESSIONALS

Japanese marketers are not professionals in a technical sense; they seem
to consider marketing too important to leave to experts. Marketing is a
concern for everybody in the organization. Every employee of the company is a marketer when interacting with the outside world. This is similar to what happens in a few odd firms in the West, like Wal-Mart,
Scandinavian Airlines System, and Ritz-Carlton. But it is the rule in Japan,
where most companies still do not have marketing managers or marketing departments.[2]

That marketing is a business for everybody in the organization, not a
professional function, is emphasized by the autobiographical reminiscences
of corporate leaders such as Akio Morita at Sony or Eiji Toyoda at Toyota,
but also by more broadly based studies.[3] The common Japanese practice of
entry-level hiring and subsequent rotation of job positions is predicated on
the lack of position-specific skills. These practices help account for the fact
that many individuals with engineering backgrounds are involved in marketing in Japanese manufacturing firms, an important factor in their marketing research, as we will see. At the same time, however, in-house training
to develop skills is extensive and continues intensively until the middle
management (*kacho*) level is reached at about age thirty-five to forty.[4] Even
though a rising number of managers are educated in marketing abroad,
and Japan is also developing business schools, the entry-level hiring practices and the development of company-specific skills in-house have made
MBAs difficult to assimilate, and they are mainly used as internationalization (*kokusaika*) catalysts, rather than as skilled professionals.[5]

Marketing by the Japanese, in Japan and overseas, is fundamentally an application of common sense. The Japanese "marketers," who carry out the marketing tasks as the West defines them, view themselves basically as amateurs when compared to their Western counterparts. They do use professional help for specific purposes, including marketing research and advertising in Western markets. But for the most part, they prefer synthesizing over analyzing, common words over professional jargon, and simplicity over sophistication. The Mazda Miata, for example, was suggested to the Japanese by a designer in California who longed for a traditional British sports car, but with Japanese functionality and quality. Mazda obliged without losing much time on market research.

Why do Japanese marketers lack professional identity compared to the marketing specialists so common in Western firms? The typical answer is that Japan does not have business schools where marketers can be trained—a feeble answer because the Japanese do send students to foreign business schools today. The explanation lies in their conception of a customer. A customer to them is a special guest, a god whose visit is the best compliment a businessman can wish for. To treat the guest right means to be simple, create good feelings, and speak in common words. But to be "professional" means setting oneself on a higher pedestal than the customer. Stories about the pampered customers in Japan are well-known also in the West.

The Japanese marketers keep close to the customers naturally. They build relationships, create loyalty, troubleshoot, and erect barriers to entry, all at the same time. You can easily visualize how this process works with industrial business-to-business products and services, where there may be few customers to keep happy. In the consumer goods markets, the Japanese use the same approach to maintain good relationships with distributors and other middlemen. As for the final consumer, the Japanese do adapt their approach and use mass media, but the ultimate marketing purpose remains the same: how to keep our guest entertained.

Much of the Japanese marketing thinking grows directly from this "simple" approach. Marketing activities such as execution of an in-store promotion may be difficult for professionals (who do not want to get their hands dirty) but come easily to amateurs. Concepts such as seeing products as "bundles of attributes" that professionals quickly grasp seem beyond the reach of amateurs. While professionals emphasize analysis and *a priori* thinking, amateurs aim for direct experience and trial and error.

This latter difference is why the Japanese, although nonprofessionals in a technical or academic sense, are actually very professional marketers. They have "savvy." In marketing, they simply trust their experience more than their book learning: Marketing is not a science, but an art or craft, perhaps. In contrast, of course, for "professional" marketers in the West, nothing substitutes for analytical learning.

INTUITION AND PROFESSIONALISM

Good professionalism means not only mastering a set of principles, but also putting those principles into action. The good doctor knows anatomy and can make the correct diagnosis. The outstanding lawyer knows the criminal code and can apply it to a particular case. The successful marketer knows how to research target-market preferences, and can translate these into the appropriate product positioning. Acting professionally means applying the guiding principles of one's profession with a cool head and objective rationality. It takes practice as well as book learning.

But what about intuition? Does not the practice of marketing, especially, but also the practice of medicine and law, require a great deal of intuitive skills, such as understanding people? A good doctor must sense a patient's mental state and how it will affect the successful progress of a course of treatment. A lawyer must intuit how a jury will react to a particular witness. Similarly, marketers must be able to predict how actual and potential customers will react to a new product or advertisement. But two aspects of marketing differentiate it from medicine and law, and together the two make professionalization suspect, if not fraudulent.

First, the purpose of marketing everywhere is to influence voluntary human behavior. "Voluntary" is important here, because medicine and law also influence human behavior. But in medicine, the principles of the profession relate to how the body reacts to a treatment, and in law the principles relate behavior to the established codes of conduct. Marketing principles attempt to relate various theories about human behavior to individual or organizational customer response. Not surprisingly, the professionalization of marketing has been accompanied by—and driven by—progress in the behavioral and social sciences attempting to predict human behavior.

If you believe that laws for human behavior exist, then you can easily accept the idea of a "science" of marketing. For others less impressed by the laws of human behavior, it is clear that marketing cannot be a science only. Rather, the successful marketer is someone with an acute sensibility and intuition for what individual customers prefer. And this sensibility leads to successful marketing campaigns by going beyond the professional marketing techniques.

Fundamentally, marketers need to predict imperfectly understood—and variable—human behavior. That's why marketing is such a people-ori-ented activity, requiring a lot of intuitive understanding. And as markets evolve, customers change their preferences. The marketer has to be able to hear and see the changes, and to adjust. The market is an arena for knowledge creation. Users and competitors don't act in a vacuum, but in specific contexts. How do you catch the concentration of a teenager play-ing Gameboy, or the frustration of a buyer trying to understand how to program a VCR? The quickest way is to be there.

A scientific approach to marketing, coupled with the technical com-plexity of the standard texts, easily distances the marketer from the mind of the customer. It also puts hard limits on the marketer's imagination—if it cannot be put into numbers, the case is harder to make. Marketing sci-ence does not mean to limit imagination, and marketing professors argue that they offer concepts that help the imagination. The gist of the profes-sors' argument is that, without concepts and words, one's eyes cannot comprehend what goes on, and no ideas will come forth. Furthermore, the marketer's judgment has to be added to the technical analysis of cus-tomers' response to marketing actions. Tacit knowledge has to be com-bined with explicit knowledge.

We agree. But the problem is that a scientific approach to marketing is not only a potential obstacle to the imagination, but it can also be very misleading by answering the wrong questions correctly. The intuition needed to transcend the technical jargon is necessarily tied to customers in specific markets and cultures. Experience, the source of much intuition, comes from specific instances, and needs the context of a new situation to be applicable. But the very nature of scientific techniques is that they are general, and can be applied in many markets. To use techniques, one needs systematic data; to exercise intuition, one needs situation-specific data. This is why the emphasis on science not only blunts intuition, but goes against it. Scientific evidence and intuitive sense should be comple-mentary, but they are often in conflict.

In this conflict, professional marketers will prefer science over intu-ition, because they can easily justify their decisions. The techniques, rather than supporting intuition, replace it. Wrong. Intuitive marketers will reject the findings. Wrong again. The two have to be in accord—the Japanese way.

Professionals divide up tasks and have people specialize in them. This is why professionalism is often defined by what one does not do—"That is not our job," "We don't do that," "I do only . . . ," and so on. Amateurs do everything. According to Japanese thinking, marketing is too impor-tant to leave to the professionals. Customers will fall through the cracks between the specializations.

SELF-RESPECT

The Japanese fondly compare their social system to a fortified wall, built of rocks of different sizes and shapes, like the walls around their castles: A strong wall needs not only big rocks but smaller ones too. And a smaller rock might well determine the strength of the wall. The Japanese quickly note that a wall in the West is usually built from uniform blocks. Furthermore, in the West blocks are worked into the predetermined shapes required in any one function. In Japan, rocks for the walls are used as they are found in nature. Similarly, company employees "belong" or "fit in" with existing employees and not within some given mold or shape.

EVERYBODY IS IMPORTANT

These differences impact human resource management directly. Even the humblest job needs to be done with care according to Japanese norms—and thus, even the humblest worker has self-respect. In the West, where the social status generally varies directly with a person's professional status and the amount of pay for the job, nonprofessional and low-paying jobs mean demoralized workers without self-respect. Not so in Japan.

When a store owner in the West enters his store he will generally walk around inspecting operations, pointing out problems, and encouraging personnel—management by walking around. He is an important man and acts as if he owns the store—which of course he does, quite literally. In Japan, by contrast, the store owner will enter, greet subordinates, and then help restock shelves, pick up trash, and take out the garbage—the meanest tasks. The message is simple—even the lowest tasks are important.[6]

This shift in perspective has many benefits:

• It makes for better worker morale. Even the meanest job merits employee self-respect.
• Managers care about employees, and will treat them as people.
• Managers understand the jobs assigned to workers.
• Most important for marketing, it affects the marketer's relationship with the customer. Not only will the customer naturally be seen as important, but the converse is also true. There is a tacit acknowledgment by the buyer of the importance of the seller's work. Buyers won't abuse sellers who try to serve, the way relationship marketing efforts can be abused in the West.

This approach is not the same as "empowerment" as we know it in the West, where workers are given a larger role in defining their jobs, or a voice in the management of their workplace. It is not delegation of authority. It is not an extrinsic reward, but a benefit that is intrinsic to the task. It is simply an acknowledgment that the job you are doing is important to the company, and if you do it well, you will be respected.

THE INVISIBLE ASSET

From the evident value of the job flows self-respect, and a desire to do it well. Amateurs becomes professionals, in the sense that the employees will try to develop their skills to the utmost. The company continually supports this effort to self-improvement by in-house courses, quality control circles, and a general *kaizen* attitude. Mistakes are tolerated, if used for constructive learning. Employees come to learn that their jobs, however insignificant they may seem at first glance, are necessary for company success.

From a marketing perspective, this approach profoundly affects the way employees deal with customers. An employee with pride in the job will learn faster and keep improving, and will be better able to help customers and listen to them with an open mind. If a mistake is made, the employee confidently focuses on helping the customer. The employee need not assign blame, but apologizes for inconveniencing the customer. The customer feels listened to, not talked at. The mistake is not explained to the customer, but rectified if at all possible.

To make this approach work, the employee's job must be interpreted broadly. These frontliners are not professionals in a narrow sense, but are responsible for more than just the immediate task at hand. While a "professional" in the West will easily delimit responsibilities, and thus be able to shift the burden of responsibility for a mistake ("It must have been a mistake by the delivery boy"), a Japanese employee is responsible for the whole function. A good—and "professional"—clothes designer also has to respond to a customer's complaints about the stitching in a dress, not hide behind salespeople. Japanese senior managers periodically have to take their turn selling company products to customers, in stores, wrapping presents, chatting with customers. It may not be done well, and thus not be "professional" in a narrow Western sense, but it is total professionalism at its best.

As product variants proliferate and customer satisfaction more and more becomes a matter of service rather than genuine product differences, the Japanese orientation toward their jobs becomes a strong competitive resource. It is an invisible asset in the true sense of the expression. The Japanese leverage off that resource, providing superior in-store prepurchase information, and superb after-sales service. There is no need for confrontation, the salespeople simply expecting the buyers to treat them as professionals, not as people with all the human frailties. There is no need for them to be defensive and try to assert themselves. This attitude, the essence of professionalism, is a powerful competitive advantage for the Japanese in many Western markets.[7]

MIKOSHI MARKETING

One way to understand how the Japanese marketers view themselves and their job is through the use of a metaphor that seems to come naturally to them. They are bearers of the company *mikoshi*, a traditional ornamented litter featured at Shinto shrine festivals. The litter supposedly carries *kamisama*, the god of the shrine, and is hoisted onto the shoulders of ten to twenty young men who are decked out in traditional half-coats (*happi* coats), sandals, and *hachimaki* headbands. The *mikoshi* has a sturdy and heavy wooden frame, the ornamentation is in gold and brass, and the *kamisama* seat is bedecked with silk clothing, fans, paper dolls, and colorful streamers. The festival-goers are treated to a parade-like display of the *mikoshi* at the climax of the festival, when the rhythmic shouts of the carriers can be heard coming down the main streets around the shrine.

The Japanese marketers naturally view the customer as the *kamisama* whom they carry on their shoulders. The *mikoshi* may represent the product and service supporting the customer, and the ornamentation and streamers represent the advertising, brand name, and promotion that the company does to help make the product attractive. To the onlookers, the colorful *mikoshi* and its ornamentation give status to the *kamisama* and the shrine. Marketers help the customer look good, which helps make the product attractive to potential customers.

The young men and women shout ("*Wasshoi! Wasshoi!*") to coordinate their movement, and rock from side to side as they parade through the crowds. The leaders are up front, the strongest ones are in the center crouched low, and others support the shafts extending beyond the wooden frame. One can easily see the metaphor: Different kinds of people are needed to serve the customer, including channel middlemen who represent extensions of the core company. Onlookers can also discern the obvious pride in the work done. The carriers are proud to carry the *kamisama*, and feel they are among the select few. They are eager to prove themselves better than the *mikoshi* from other shrines by parading longer, singing harder, and having more spirited carriers—but above all, by having a better constructed, more richly ornamented, and more color-ful *mikoshi*. All for the glory of the *kamisama*.

This kind of traditional ceremony has long been a part of growing up in Japan, and it transfers well into company life. New employees are treated to the company credo, taught the company song, and given the company lapel pin, and become members of the company family. Rather than focusing on personal success, they work together toward the collective goal of carrying the customer/*kamisama*.

FORCED MOTIVATION?

A note of caution needs to be inserted here, however. The egoless atten-tion to *kamisama* is not the only driver of the Japanese marketers' efforts. They work weekends, stay long hours to satisfy a client, accept overseas assignments away from their families, treat business as a matter of discipline, and never allow themselves to think that the victory is won, that the job is done. But it is also their lack of choices in their private and working lives that makes the Japanese so dedicated.

The lack of choices is all-pervasive, but in particular it means that when you start with one company, that is it. You are stuck. There is little you can do in the way of changing to another company, unless you are ready to risk your family's and your own happiness, at no discernible advantage. Leaving is always a negative choice, the few times it happens: because the company went bankrupt, because you could not get along with your boss, because you refused to leave your family in Japan and go to Africa alone for three years.

The reasons for this state of affairs are well-known. Hiring at entry lev-els only, creation of a unique company culture where latecomers cannot contribute, lifetime employment, and a lack of mobility in labor markets are closely interrelated factors. Why is the mobility factor so important? Because of the lack of mobility, the individual's and the company's aim will always coincide. What is good for the company is good for the indi-vidual. When the company succeeds, the individual succeeds. When the company fails, the individual fails as well. When promoting someone over you is in the best interest of the firm, it is in your best interest too. There can naturally be some bitter feelings, yes—but this is only foolish selfishness. If the company benefits with your competitive colleague at the top, so do you. So he is not really your enemy but your friend—and as you must accept defeat, so he must compensate you for his victory. Conflict is all in the family—figuratively and often literally.

But why join a company at all? Are there not other ways to make a liv-ing, raise a family, live a life? Start something by yourself? By and large, for the majority of Japanese, the answer is no. Companies in Japan exist, precisely, to offer jobs for the people. They are not confused, as Western companies increasingly are, by thinking that companies exist solely for shareholders, or even for customers who need the products. Companies in Japan exist for the employees, to create acceptable living conditions for the employees, who are certainly better off than they were after the war.

The recent recession has sparked a vigorous debate on the issue of shareholder versus employee rights in Japan.[8] The obligation toward the employees goes a long way in explaining why layoffs are still so relatively uncommon in Japan. It also makes their reengineering efforts focus on placing people in more productive work rather than firing them.

For Japanese businessmen, satisfying shareholders is still a minor constraint, necessary to attract new money. More strikingly, making products or providing services is only what businesses do, and not why they exist. Manufacturing products is like eating, and satisfying shareholders is like sleeping: both are necessary, but hardly the reason for a business. And by themselves, they do not explain the behavior of companies and their employees.

No, the crystal-clear link between the self-interest and the company interest is the driving factor. This linkage, as codified in the semiannual bonuses that are tied to company performance, was identified early on as a key ingredient in Japanese successes—Abegglen's first book documented it, for example.[9] The basic idea is of course similar to stock incentives and related end-of-year bonuses in the West—but the powerful impact in Japan derives to a large extent from the lack of other employment options.

The company is like an extended family. You may not like your colleagues, but you don't choose your relatives. You may not like your job, but your role was defined when you arrived. Once your company agrees to a business relationship with a supplier, it is assumed to last forever, like a marriage. Economic considerations are important, but, like eating and sleeping, not the prime reasons for existing, and certainly not sufficient reason for divorce.

The best part of the lack of choice is, of course, that you are not continuously having to reevaluate your decision and second-guess the intentions of others. You are stuck—so are they. Let's concentrate on the business at hand. Bonding occurs naturally; there is little need for well-formulated strategic plans that cannot be implemented—if you know what has to be done, do it; if not, let's talk about it. And talk. And talk. Because this is not just business—it is what life with relatives consists of. Talk. They have very little private time. No wonder if some Japanese salarymen go nuts or die from *karosi* (overwork).

COMPANY AGAINST EMPLOYEES

Western employees, managers as well as workers, might scoff at such sacrifice for the good of the company. But this misses the quid pro quo that is implicit in the relationship between company success and job security in Japanese corporations.

In the West, cost cutting and reengineering have made companies successful at the expense of employees. In traditional industries, company success is today more likely to lead to unemployment than to new hires. As workers are laid off and managers dismissed in the wake of mergers and acquisitions, companies beholden to stockholders treat employees as the proverbial punched card, people being "folded, spindled, and mutilated."

Despite increasing pressure from international investors and financial markets, the Japanese companies are still in the business of providing work for their employees, not simply offering a high return to stockholders. Good managers lead and help workers to be efficient; layoffs represent management failure. People are the real assets of a company; dismissing employees means getting rid of experience and know-how. Yes, even Japanese companies reengineer, but they avoid laying off people.

2

SATISFYING CUSTOMERS

How many times have you felt the satisfaction-guaranteed promise had a hollow ring to it? How many times has it seemed downright phony? The Japanese have a solution for this: They never guarantee satisfaction. They just do their best, hope for it, and are happy if it happens. If this sounds quaint and old-fashioned, so be it.

For the Japanese a guarantee of satisfaction is like stepping on someone's soul, an intrusion of privacy. What makes the marketers think that they can satisfy the customers? Who are the sellers to judge whether the customers are really satisfied? Are the sellers God? "Satisfaction guaranteed" is a statement of hubris, of unforgivable pride. The Japanese conception is that the buyer is God, and that the marketers are the servant of God—if God accepts them.

This conception of the customer and of customer satisfaction underlying Japanese marketing practices has been developed in the fiercely competitive Japanese home market. It involves both cultural and economic factors.

WHO IS A CUSTOMER?

The tradition of individualism preoccupies Western marketers with individual behavior. Customers are individuals, whether they act as a member of a family, an organization, or an ethnic group. The various social factors pressuring the purchase decision effectively constrain the individual's freedom to act.

THE CONSUMER AS AN INDIVIDUAL

Where the Western assumption is that all people prefer "freedom," the Japanese view of human behavior is that all people would prefer to "belong." This view has colored their marketing effort, at home and overseas.

Treating the consumers as independent decision makers should lead to greater respect for their integrity. It does, but when coupled with an assumed equality between buyers and sellers, the exchange easily becomes a power-based bargaining game, to see who can get most of the pie. It is a zero-sum game, not a win-win situation. What one gains, the other has to give up. This in turn naturally leads to manipulation. Marketers are led to find angles and hidden motives to exploit buyers and overcome buyer resistance, and consumers in turn distrust dealers and manufacturers. The advice from magazines such as *Consumer Reports* for consumers to arm themselves with figures on the markups and margins the auto dealers work with provides a good illustration—the transaction becomes a political power game.[10] It is perhaps not so surprising that a company such as Saturn has scored major share gains in the very competitive U.S. car market by providing not a superior automobile, but a fixed-price, no-hassle purchasing situation.

The stress on freedom and individualism in the West actually serves to reinforce the manufacturers' position. Respecting someone's integrity easily spills over into a buyer-beware sentiment. "Treat customers as adults" becomes a code for "offer nothing." And when a buyer or a seller wants to act altruistically and care for the other party, that party may interpret the act as subtle manipulation and abrogation of rights. In the current telecommunications warfare among AT&T, MCI, and Sprint, a take-no-prisoners battle for customers, cash and free calls are inducements to get customers to change carriers. The companies even provide postcards to send to competing carriers to stop their telemarketing calls, "protecting" their customers from competition, in fact asking customers to give up the benefits of choice.

What has gone wrong? How can the zero-sum game be turned into the win-win situation to which so many salespeople pay lip service? Part of the answer is simple and straightforward. In economic reality, the manufacturer gains by satisfying the customers, and the customers gain if they help the firm do this. The firm must work harder to learn more about what the consumers want, but the consumers must also make an effort and help provide that information. This situation is the ideal in Japan, where many firms and their customers more or less implicitly contract into partnerships through buyer loyalty and company product development efforts. It is also the situation in some high-tech industries, such as

PC software, where highly involved customers provide a testing ground for new products.[11] The Japanese marketplace provides a beta-testing proving ground for many new Japanese products.

Stressing the mutuality of the relationship between sellers and buyers helps the Japanese avoid some of the manipulative aspects of Western marketing. The company's products and services enable the customer—and the customer's patronage ensures the company's continued operation. As in life: Social groups constrain individuals, but they also make people belong. Family ties, while encumbering, also create opportunities. A society's norms may prohibit certain actions, but also help to accomplish tasks that individuals cannot complete otherwise. When homework is a class project, a delinquent student will be helped immediately by classmates. Company allegiance, while limiting mobility and narrowing perspectives, creates a comfort zone in which to feel accepted.

Companies use the idea of group allegiance to create value-added options for their customers. Canon camera owners are invited to join clubs that offer weekend trips to photogenic sites, a magazine, and special rebates on accessories. Yamaha piano buyers who join a club are offered various levels of training programs by Yamaha-certified teachers. Overseas, the companies tread more softly, but try to create a sentiment among their customers that they belong to a special group. This is the same philosophy that induced Saturn to invite its customers to a huge party at its Missouri plant in 1995, memorialized in its TV commercials. Japanese marketers believe fervently that their best advertising is good word-of-mouth from satisfied owners—but, more than that, every person using their product in fact advertises it. And the Japanese don't want their products left somewhere, broken down, where people can see them. If a Honda employee sees a Honda on the side of the road, abandoned, the employee will try to find a way to have the vehicle towed.

The Japanese approach sidesteps individualism to focus on establishing a mutually supportive relationship between buyer and seller. Does this sound patronizing to you? It should. For the Japanese, the concept of a strong relationship between two perfectly free and independent individuals is an impossible dream. There must be accommodation of the other party, some yielding of one's absolute independence, some creation of dependence; otherwise no relationship exists. This accommodation governs the Japanese treatment of their customers.

THE EXCHANGE IS NOT BETWEEN EQUALS

The win-win perspective is reinforced by the way Japanese conceive of transactions: They are hierarchical, not horizontal exchanges.

Western marketing typically views its principal task as one of effecting exchanges among like-minded individuals, a negotiation. The exchange perspective received particularly strong credence with the seminal Bagozzi (1978) article, which detailed the philosophical underpinnings of the concept. According to Bagozzi, marketing transactions are "arm's-length," meaning they are based on the intrinsic benefits of the exchange to selfishly motivated individuals, not on any sense of altruism or kinship. No party is forced to transact, and each is free to withdraw at any time.

To Japanese marketers, this concept is too balanced, too strong an expression of democracy, too much a relationship between equals—in essence, too unreal and unnatural. In Japan, the buyer with money is the master, the one with a product or service to sell is the servant. There is exchange, to be sure—but only at the mercy of the buyer. The reason for the inequality is clear to the Japanese: The seller is always ready and willing to exchange with any buyer, but the buyer is not always willing to buy from any seller.[12] The customer has the power.

Even though obviously contingent on culture, the difference is seen by the Japanese as intrinsic to the economics of the exchange process. Any seller is, to them, in a weak spot——unless, of course, the seller is a monopolist. When the roles shift in that direction, as they did in the past in Japanese government services such as railroads, the service level decreases dramatically, and the arrogance of the trainmasters rises commensurately. Only the Shinkansen bullet trains, which attract foreigners and are the showcase for the railroads, maintain some semblance of the typically high Japanese service levels.

The view of the seller below the buyer is not clear in the Western literature on economic exchange because of our democratic ideal of individuals as equals. It is not politically correct. But in notions like "the consumer is king," "the customer is always right," and so on, the inequality notion is clearly embodied. Thus, the Japanese sentiment is not necessarily against Western notions, although as we saw in chapter 1, they prefer the godlike *kamisama* or, in daily speech, *okyakusama* (honored guest) rather than the less spiritual king. How does the hierarchical view with buyers on top of sellers solve the zero-sum problem? It leads naturally to attention and service for the buyer, to pampering the customer. Is this not manipulative and insincere? Yes, of course it is—but it is obviously so, and needs no excuse. There is no pretense of equality, neither one of sincerity or brotherhood—the seller is a servant. But this also requires some yielding on the part of the buyer, so as not to pressure the seller for any and all concessions. This means that price is usually not negotiable, and that prices on similar goods are comparable. With price competition increasing, as is happening with the new discount outlets emerging under foreign pressure, gradual changes in the Japanese companies' treatment of their consumers can already be seen.

THE CUSTOMER IS NOT ALWAYS RIGHT

A standard injunction to which lip service is paid in Western marketing is that "the customer is always right." With the attention of the Japanese on inequality, one would think that they were prime exponents of this dogma. Such is not the case, however, for a very simple reason: Who is right or wrong is a completely irrelevant issue.

When a customer returns the expensive drink in the hotel bar because "I ordered a different drink," the waiter neither argues nor hesitates: Sound business reason demands that the waiter take the drink back. In Japan the waiter does. (Much of recent customer satisfaction research suggests that the same policy could benefit a Western setting.) When the consumer claims that the appliance does not work, the service shop will not doubt or interrogate her, but promptly repair or replace the appliance. When the buyer does not like the way his new shoes fit, a shoe salesperson will help him fix the problem rather than make him feel like a nuisance. Both being intelligent people, the customer knows that he is a nuisance, and is grateful to the clerk for not rubbing it in.[13]

This thinking permeates Japanese marketing in more fundamental ways as well. Most Japanese salespeople are sufficiently well-educated about the products they sell to advise a customer, "Maybe this model would be better than the one you asked for," or "Don't let movie stars' pictures trick you—the hairstyle you mentioned is not good for the kind of life you live," or "There is no need to buy such an expensive racket unless you play more than five times a week." The automobile salesperson will learn everything about the customer and then select the best car for the client. Such a "consulting" sales job is both necessary and natural since the buyer will hold the company and the salesperson responsible if the car does not work out to the buyer's satisfaction.

Once the seller's insistence on equality with the buyer is given up, a new mindset naturally emerges: The buyer feels more satisfied and more willing to cede power to the seller, and to let the seller's often superior knowledge guide the choices. After all, the king (or even the *kamisama*) does not know everything. The seller can assume an advisory role, forget about maintaining self-pride, and really serve the customer. When the customer recognizes that there is genuine assistance forthcoming, not simply cheerfulness and faked friendship a la "friend of the family," the customer will also be more forgiving. Mistakes are not cause for acrimonious debate, but are handled in good spirits.

Once the relationship is tilted to being one of the "king's advisers," the seller will also not talk down to an uninformed customer. The king is of course not an expert in all things. Thus a more informative dialogue is possible, with the customer willing to ask simpler questions without being embarrassed by the seller. The seller, in turn, must translate technical jargon into useful, everyday language to address the user's problem.

CUSTOMER LOYALTY

The best Japanese companies push this culture-based logic further. The close attention to customers' needs, coupled with a willingness to improve continuously (the well-known *kaizen* principle) becomes the true competitive advantage of the company. Instead of statically viewing its core competencies, the company helps its royal customers "dream the future," or "create life," to use some typical Japanese expressions. This kind of pledge from the company guides the best Japanese (and, increasingly, the best Western) companies. Kyocera, a supplier of semiconductor ceramics to many high-tech companies, calls it "following the customer's way of thinking." For Kyocera, the customer's bottom line is the ultimate customer satisfaction score.

One benefit of the ensuing bonding between buyer and seller is a higher than usual degree of brand and store loyalty, the buyer preferring his "trusted aide." Bonding also raises higher barriers to entry, blocking foreign entrants into the Japanese market.

In this situation, a deeper relationship forms quite naturally. Customers stay closer to sellers, more loyal to salespeople and to trusted brands. The customers can be demanding but not aggressive; they simply expect more from the sellers than a take-it-or-leave-it attitude. The seller now has the added responsibility not only to satisfy requests, but also to suggest new alternatives. The king's advisers try to anticipate questions and needs by talking with their king, and by using their own expertise and imagination to generate alternatives. Accepting a subordinate role in fact allows the seller to exercise a greater repertory to establish mutual recognition and a personally satisfying relationship. In a horizontal exchange between equals, each player must match every move by the counterpart, easily digressing into an I-win–you-lose gaming situation where partners become opponents. By accepting the basic inequality in positions—the seller has to allow anyone to buy, the buyer can choose among sellers—both parties can accept their respective responsibilities. A king has responsibilities vis-à-vis his subordinates, and even a seller is frequently a customer or "god" when away from his job.

PERSONAL SELLING

The philosophy that the seller is below the buyer makes the Japanese salesperson approach a personal selling situation differently than a Western salesperson, either at home or abroad. The sustained application of this cultural factor distinguishes the successful Japanese salesperson's behavior from that of the traditional hard-driving Western salesman.

JAPANESE SALESMANSHIP

Even if the West grasps the subordinated role of the seller in principle, the person actually selling retains his own "pride" as a human being, based on the cultural belief that an individual, in the role of employee in a company, still enjoys the rights and privileges accorded him as an individual. In this respect the Japanese differ. For the given working hours, the Japanese employee has in effect sold a certain time of his life to the company, forfeiting the right to fill these work hours with personal matters—a kind of Faustian bargain, with the company in the role of Mephistopheles. Department store clerks do not banter about their personal lives, vacations, boyfriends, or holiday plans as you often hear in American department stores. Have store employees in the United States ever treated you like an intruder on their intimate conversation? This situation is totally unacceptable in Japan: The employees are company property once their job starts, and must conduct themselves accordingly or be ostracized from their work group.[14]

With interpersonal skills among the Japanese very finely developed at home, and with language skills very difficult for a foreigner to master, it is not surprising that most foreign companies doing business in Japan are forced to hire Japanese salespeople and sales representatives. The other side of the coin is that with the lack of international education at home, the Japanese salesperson going abroad rarely has the requisite skills for handling contract negotiations, in-store service requests, and so on. Personal selling as a rule has to be localized for even the most global of corporations and industries.

EGO AND PRIDE

One advantage of the Japanese approach over Western ways is that no ego enters the salesperson's interaction with the customer. The salesperson takes complaints, remarks, or requests at face value and tries to understand exactly what the customer wants.

This lack of ego is one reason that the Japanese seem so unemotional in sales meetings and negotiations. They are rarely "fired up," and certainly don't believe that they should be excited in the presence of a customer. They want ice, not fire, in the belly. If you cannot come to agreement without a hard-sell argument, then wait. The good Japanese salesperson presents all the useful information about the product, but avoids drawing conclusions for the prospect, exactly opposite of the typical training for the American salesperson, whose pitch usually drives home the "only logical conclusion."

By contrast, the Western salesperson takes personal responsibility for satisfying the customer. Not surprisingly, the interaction then often becomes a contest of wills, where the salesperson attempts to convince the potential buyer about what the buyer *really* needs.

From the Japanese viewpoint, for salespeople to let their own conviction play a role is exactly the wrong tactic to take. It actually plays against them, because the salespeople become the equals—or even the superiors—of the customers. It has the same effect as slapping the customer's shoulder. To say to the king "I think this will fit better" suggests that you are at least his equal, and that your opinion matters to him. Wait at least until your opinion is solicited. Of course, you are doing what you think is good for the customer—and good for yourself. As usual, it goes without saying.[15]

This concept generates quite a different attitude in personal selling in Japan. In the West, store clerks customarily treat a customer as someone who needs help, and who therefore is being done a favor. This treatment misses the point that basically the customer has already done the seller a big favor (namely coming to the store) and that the customer might be induced to do the even bigger favor of parting with money and actually buying something. In Japan shoppers are greeted with the words "Welcome—thank you for coming to our store" rather than the democratic "May I help you?" heard in the United States. In a sense the difference is natural. How could democratic Americans know how to greet a king? Many would perhaps rather not know.

Paradoxically, and contrary to what one might think at first blush, the yielding of the equality constraint in an interpersonal selling situation allows the seller to gain pride in the product. Japanese sellers have genuine pride in the integrity of their product offering, much more so than many Western marketers.[16] This reflects the Japanese product orientation. Where a Western marketer views the selling situation as a semiconfrontational occasion, in which it is important to show oneself confident and trustworthy, the Japanese focus on the product offering. Personalities matter little, and, for the Japanese, when the egos start coming into the picture, doubt is immediately cast upon the integrity of the product and firm. American sales management strategy tends to overemphasize presentation techniques and individual skills. The Japanese try to make the product sell itself, with the salesperson unimportant.

DON'T TAKE IT PERSONALLY!

This aspect of the buyer-seller relationship is what ultimately does in individualism in personal selling. The insistence on personal involvement and thus ego leads the sellers to overestimate their own importance, and induces them to "lead" the customers—asking questions, probing answers, and in other ways placing themselves as the "doctors," the customers as the "patients." This is also why professionalism in personal service is a killer—it creates the sense that the seller is above the buyer rather than the other way around. Small wonder that most shoppers feel stepped on in stores—they are.

The sacrifice for the American salesperson who tries to adopt the Japanese mode is not as great as it might first appear. It is just that the tendency of the Americans to personify the sales situation—"I am the company, I stand behind the product"—which is assumed to create pride in the product sold, instead places too strong an emphasis on the individual salesperson's ego. His pride is at stake, a failure is taken as a personal failure, and a concluded agreement is a victory for the individual. The Japanese salesperson is different, not so ego-involved with the product and the company, paradoxically even though he is the company even more than the American salesperson. The company backs him fully, and failure and success are not a function of individual performance in a particular negotiation. Thus there is no justification for him to get too excited about the successful conclusion of a given sale. If he does he is inviting disaster. One day he will get angry with a customer, and say something as an individual, person to person. The ensuing loss of face for him and his company would be unforgivable.

In the end, this all means that the Japanese are not working with "fire in their bellies." Americans want to rally around the flag to get going to compete against whomever, thinking that the personal "ownership" of a cause is the key to success. It is, perhaps, in a Western setting. But nothing could be further from the practice in companies in Japan, where discipline is everything. The Japanese employees don't compete with fire, but with ice, in their stomachs.

CUSTOMER SATISFACTION

Given their views of who a customer is—and who a marketer is—the Japanese approach to customer satisfaction is naturally different from that in the West. Even though they tend to take a more qualitative and less quantitative view of satisfaction ("more is less" is their motto with customer satisfaction figures), they nevertheless score higher than most Western competitors. And when winning the numbers game becomes important, they approach the job with their usual attention to detail and focus on the real situation. We will talk more about their market research in the next chapter, but should mention briefly that the Japanese automakers were the ones who first told dealers to focus on the items covered in the usual J. D. Power satisfaction survey. They also invented the idea of asking all their customers to give the highest rating, or else to explain what was wrong so the dealer could correct it and then receive the highest ranking. Not to be outdone, dealerships for Western cars today admonish customers that "only excellent is acceptable," somewhat of a bastardization of the Japanese approach.

CREATING SATISFACTION

For the Japanese, customer satisfaction is subtle. First, even though functional quality of products and services is sometimes difficult for the average consumer to evaluate, sooner or later quality compromises will translate into malfunctioning. Thus, to cut corners and compromise on details is suicide (and not even an honorable hara-kiri), especially since competition is likely to offer an attractive alternative choice. Consequently, all or most Japanese-made products fulfill the basic performance requirements very well. But at the same time, the idea that reliability, durability, flexibility, and similar functional attributes would be sufficient for satisfaction is unacceptable to the Japanese. Thus, to them, a customer's performance expectations of a product relate not simply to the quality of the functional aspects of a product but to a kind of emotional and aesthetic satisfaction. It is not difficult for a customer to evaluate a product or a service—it is simply the creation of a state of mind. In the end, products and services, say the Japanese, are means to create the perfect state of mind.[17]

SATISFACTION AND QUALITY

The Japanese thinking about customer satisfaction (CS) relates closely to their view of quality. The quality control circles, the zero defects, and the total quality control (TQC) concepts are well-known, of course. In terms of quality from a customer viewpoint, the Japanese distinguish between functional quality (*atarimae hinshitsu*) and emotional quality (*miryoku teki hinshitsu*). Functional quality is largely a product of manufacturing and its zero-defects emphasis, and is assumed to be taken for granted by the Japanese customer. The emotional ("feel good") quality refers to more subjective criteria, including brand image, status, and style.[18] Since Japanese companies are generally very competitive in terms of product design, engineering, and manufacturing, the competitive edge of a company tends to be found in these softer factors.

The CS activities that yield high satisfaction involve high scores on the emotional quality factors. If the company excels here, not only does satisfaction and therefore retention go up, but the possibility of imitation by competitors is low. By contrast, high scores on the functional quality dimensions matter relatively less, since these factors are taken for granted. But low functional quality scores can really hurt by creating dissatisfaction—while low emotional quality hurts relatively less. These relationships are depicted in Exhibit 2:1.

Exhibit 2:1
Customer Satisfaction and Two Kinds of Quality

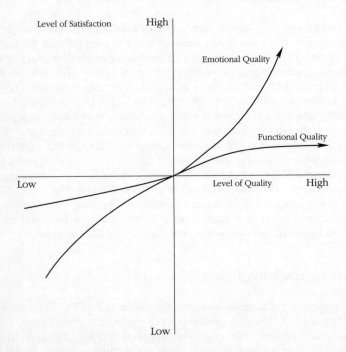

THE SONY EXPERIENCE
An example can be used to illustrate how this thinking has influenced companies' CS activities. It comes from Sony, a leader in CS activity

among the larger well-known companies.[19] Sony's CS activities illustrate the depth of rethinking that is necessary to truly implement a CS philosophy.

From 1987 to 1989 Sony's "quality in manufacturing" program lowered its manufacturing defect rate for components, subassemblies, and finished products from 3 percent to the targeted 1 percent rate. But product breakdowns after purchase did not decrease: From the customer's viewpoint nothing had changed. Zero-defect manufacturing was not sufficient for improving product quality in use.

Consequently, in 1989 the company enlarged its zero-defects (ZD) project to focus on the customer, and renamed it "Reliability ZD." In addition, Sony created a new slogan, "Does it satisfy the customer?" to launch a program of cultural change within the corporation. Obliterating any NIH (not invented here) syndrome, Sony even invited the Japanese head of operations at Tokyo Disneyland to lecture on satisfying customers. The success of the Disney transplant, especially its ability to identify critical customer-pleasing elements of its operations, interested a number of Japanese companies, not only in the service sector.

How could Sony make the CS concept more real to its employees? It first expanded the notion of a "customer" beyond the person buying the company's products to all suppliers, agents, distributors, and retailers with whom Sony employees came into contact. Then, even more important, a "customer" was redefined as any person whom an employee contacted or passed in the course of the job. "Treat *everyone* as a customer, and you will build quality into our product and service" was and remains the thinking.

Today, Sony regards as "customer" even those other Sony employees—bosses, subordinates, colleagues, and so on—with whom the employee comes into daily contact. Sony developed and internally disseminated the chart in Exhibit 2:2 to demonstrate the various relationships between an employee and all customers.

The company also developed a sensitivity training program for its employees. The aim was to demonstrate to the employees how traditional habits needed to change and to teach a new attitude. The program, still active, takes the participants through three stages.

First stage: Products and after-sales service are treated as separate. This stage explains the pros and cons of keeping products and after-sales service separate, the traditional practice (and what Sony used to do). This stage involves seminar-style interactions and lectures. It is meant to set up the straw man against which the new practices can be contrasted, and to allow questions and counter objections from personnel with long experience.

Exhibit 2:2
Sony: Who Are Your Customers?

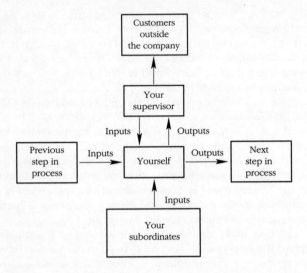

Second stage: In the second stage, the notion of integrating product
and service is put forward. The participants are exposed to the advantages of having service considerations adopted in the product design and
manufacturing phases. Company personnel demonstrate and exemplify
the change of mindset necessary to adopt the integrative perspective. For
example, designers and engineers whose projects have been affected by
service considerations and customer input are asked to "show and tell"
about their experiences.

Third stage: The third stage involves the bridging of the gap between
company and customer by the adoption of a pro-customer attitude. This
is new to Sony, and the program involves speakers from other companies, academic experts, and workshops and role-playing sessions. The
program attempts to create a new core attitude among the participants,
one that makes the employees automatically adopt a customer perspective in all activities. Even though Japanese have long been trained to listen carefully to others, company members who are not in daily contact
with outside customers are not used to viewing their own jobs from others' perspectives. By redefining the customer to include also people
inside the company, Sony attempts to grow the pro-consumer attitude
throughout the organization.

Exhibit 2:3 shows visually the process involved.

Exhibit 2:3
Customer Satisfaction

	Quality of
1st Step	Product *or* Service
2nd Step	Product *and* Service
3rd Step	——————— Attitude ——————— Product *and* Service *and* Behavior

To make the three-stage process tangible, the example of the redesign of the Walkman product and the illustration in Exhibit 2:4 are instructive. Originally about two-thirds of the Walkman repairs were due to customers accidentally dropping the units while running. At first, Sony interpreted these accidents as a service problem, and treated them under standard warranty conditions.

Exhibit 2:4
Customer Satisfaction

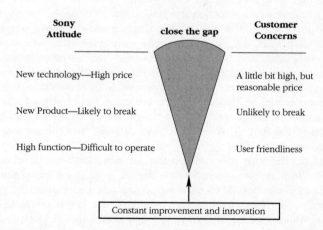

Sony Attitude	close the gap	Customer Concerns
New technology—High price		A little bit high, but reasonable price
New Product—Likely to break		Unlikely to break
High function—Difficult to operate		User friendliness

Constant improvement and innovation

But as the salespeople fed information back to production, Sony managers realized that the accidents should be seen as a product design problem. Consequently, a design and engineering team redesigned the Walkman case, using corrugated plastic material, with a contoured surface, and extra slits for belts, so that the unit would less likely be dropped.

However, as the product design became more obviously targeted toward an active lifestyle, buyers in turn began using the Walkman for aerobics and various sports activities. The rate of accidental drops did not come down as expected, but showed even a slight increase, resulting in increased and costly warranty claims. Sony management had a choice: either limit the coverage under warranty and make sure that the customers understood those limits, or do another redesign. The company opted for the latter, because, as the design team leader said, customers must be provided with products that do not restrict their activity. This is an extension of the principle that products should be maximally easy to use, a tenet of the quality movement. Sony wants its products to open up new uses and enable users to do things they could not do before.

It was back to the drawing board. Using new materials and employing automobile body construction know-how, designers made the new Walkman units strong enough to withstand most physical abuse and any accidental drop. Although accidents still happen, warranty claims are down significantly, and customer satisfaction is higher than before.

Sony's other CS actions have followed more traditional lines. In addition to increasing the use of customer feedback surveys, the company has also created a special product laboratory to test new products in a more extreme environment than users would normally encounter. The company has rewritten instruction manuals to reflect usage needs and cut the typical technical jargon and instituted a "customers' days" program four times each year, during which senior corporate managers answer customer complaints and become more sensitive to customer needs. In the typical Japanese tradition, the company also collects and rewards essays on CS improvements from its employees. Sony received more than two thousand entries in 1989 alone! The company has published a book on its CS activities, titling it *CS 1.0.0*, where the "1" stands for "best care for everyone," the first "0" stands for "zero defects," and the second "0" for "zero complaints."

Judging from the Sony case, what is the difference between developing high quality and creating customer satisfaction? A quality focus is fundamentally inward-directed. It focuses on people and processes inside the organization, and treats customers as outsiders, not key players. As we saw in the Walkman case, this inward focus affects things like product design. Western companies easily fall into the trap of thinking quality of product rather than satisfaction of customers. For example, NBD, a Canadian-based manufacturer of high-quality stereo amplifiers and tuners, offers an automatic muting of the sound as its units are turned on, "to protect the speakers from sudden soundbursts." But this means that there is an extra key to switch off when turning on the unit, and modern speakers don't need the feature. Despite customer and dealer complaints, the company insists on keeping the feature, because it is "a distinguishing advantage of NBD." It is also important to note, perhaps, that the feature is the invention of the company owner himself.

Such self-serving attitudes are anathema to the Japanese. Quality is nothing if it constrains the customer. A customer satisfaction focus must place the customers squarely in the middle of the strategy, as final arbiters of the level of quality achieved. The shift is from a "quality produced" focus to a "quality delivered" perspective. This is why Sony has gone to such pains to redefine what it is doing (see Exhibit 2:5). The very *language* used inside the organization should be that of the customer, not that of the company.

Exhibit 2:5
Culture Gap

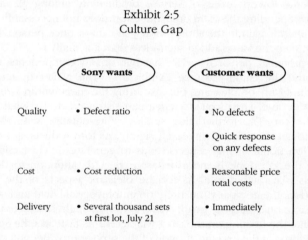

	Sony wants	Customer wants
Quality	• Defect ratio	• No defects • Quick response on any defects
Cost	• Cost reduction	• Reasonable price total costs
Delivery	• Several thousand sets at first lot, July 21	• Immediately

SATISFACTION AND PERSONAL SERVICE

Western marketers commonly distinguish between products and services; the Japanese distinguish also between *personal* service, such as a restaurant, and *embodied* services, such as cash machines and vending machines. In the West, voice mail and automated response technology might yield a gain in efficiency and actually be an improvement on the incompetent customer representatives some firms employ. The Japanese marketers are more old-fashioned, and use person-to-person contacts and interpersonal skills as crucial tools to generate customer satisfaction.

As managers everywhere recognize, there are services in products and products in services. Camera manufacturers need to offer dealer training and after-sales service. Banks can offer credit cards and cash machines.

The important distinction is not whether the business as a whole fits into a "products" or "service" classification, but simply which value-generating activity is sold as a product ("embodied services" as an economist would say), and which relies on personal interaction with the customer. For the Japanese, the management of the two parts differs in style, content, and complexity.

Japanese personal service is characterized by extreme indulgence, infinite patience, sympathetic listening, and quick response to demands. The aim is to spoil the customer. A common complaint of Americans returning from Tokyo is the lack of service in the United States—while, on the other hand, the returning Japanese expatriates (who often miss the freedom and expanse of the West) marvel at how comfortable they feel in Japan. While the caretaking may well make Japanese service the best, Japan also has one of the lowest levels of service productivity among all developed nations.[20] Spending the extra time and effort does not necessarily translate into economic gain in the short run. If you cannot price personal services directly, then the value added seems less than it actually is.

Like products, personal service has two quality components, the functional and the emotional (see Exhibit 2:6). The waiter in a restaurant should not only be pleasant, but also bring the meal within a reasonable amount of time. The nice auto repairman also needs to fix what is wrong with the car. The forthcoming service representative with the airline needs to get the ticket changed efficiently. As for products, a breakdown in the functional quality aspects tends to generate dissatisfaction, while getting the job done is more or less expected. Attention to detail and manuals plays a big role. As for the pleasant aspects of the personal interaction, the company must rely on employee initiative and individual skill. Emotional service quality can generate high satisfaction scores, much like the frosting on the cake will accent its taste. As the Sony manual suggests, in the end the attitude of the service provider will determine the customer's level of satisfaction (see Exhibit 2:2 again).

Exhibit 2:6
Four Quality Components

	Product or "Embodied" Service	Personal Service
Functional Quality (Objective)	Zero defects	Competence (what you do)
Emotional Quality (Subjective)	Brand image	Manner (what you say and how you say it)

PERSONAL SERVICE IS FREE

To Professor Keizaburo Asai at Keio University in Tokyo, one fundamental difference from the Western conception of marketing is that in Japan personal service is, or should be, free.[21] Tipping someone who provides a personal service is an insult in a culture still dominated by a suppression of individual gain and sacrifice for the common good. It also brings out the fundamental instrumentality of the service, crudely reducing the transaction to mere business. Gift giving is a much more acceptable solution, with a function that resembles tipping (payment for a job well-done or to be done), but avoids the calculation of a monetary price (although the gift has to be commensurate with the status of the persons and the magnitude of the task at hand, a judgment that requires some expertise).[22]

The desire to avoid transparency is pervasive. If charging for a service is unavoidable, then the seller offers compensation. The car salesperson gives a birthday present to his customer's young son, a new bank customer receives a present in the mail (and the branch office will send someone to pick up deposits or return with funds withdrawn).

Naturally, if something goes wrong with a newly purchased household appliance, the store will send an employee to pick up the appliance and deliver it repaired or replaced. The typical Western response of "Bring it in and we'll fix it, don't worry!" is much too seller-oriented. As for big industrial purchases, if there are problems getting a machine to work or a turnkey operation to run smoothly, payments may be canceled and the contract revoked. Such business practices affect foreign suppliers more, since they increase the barriers to entry. When a new paper plant for a Japanese customer was installed by a Swedish concern a few years back, it took more than a year to solve language and technical problems and to get the plant to operate at capacity—and the customer made no payments during that time.

The cultural predisposition against paying for a service makes it difficult for the Japanese people to pay full price for most services. Predictably, the natural reaction among service providers in Japan has been to provide peripheral products for which they can charge with impunity, and also to price very high when the cultural acceptance exists. Credit cards carry interest rates that in the West would be usurious—30 percent is not impossible. Drinks at some hotel and restaurant establishments carry stratospheric price tags, not only for the foreign visitor. Telephone charges from Japan to the United States are still several times greater than in the opposite direction.

Sometimes the practice takes on a slightly unethical character from a Western perspective. Doctors and physicians, for example, often feel unable to charge a full price for examinations and diagnoses. As a consequence, their services are artificially cheap when compared to those in Western countries. The doctors get a measure of satisfaction, however, from running their own hospitals and pharmacies, taking a cut on all beds assigned and all drugs sold. Some doctors in Japan, not surprisingly, prescribe a lot of drugs for their patients. Golf and ski instructors insist that students buy all necessary equipment for their lessons in their shops. Music teachers suggest to their students specific models and stores for buying an instrument on which they get a kickback from the salesperson, their "comrade in arms." Private universities pay low salaries, but allow their faculty members to tutor private students for the entrance exams, which might be graded by the same professors.[23]

Since service providers might face some difficulty in charging a customer directly, many of the independent service businesses subcontract to other businesses. Taxi companies sign long-term contracts with a company to get steady business even though rates are lower. Many personal service vendors survive on their proximity to a big corporate complex. Around the Tokyo headquarters of Dentsu, the giant advertising agency, there is a so-called Dentsu village of service producers, from coffee houses, restaurants, and barbers to creative boutiques and printing plants. As in the West, department stores use independent trucking firms to deliver merchandise. Most of Japan's relatively few independent lawyers work on a retainer with one large corporation. Although these cooperative arrangements have their distinct counterparts in other countries, they are perhaps particularly prominent in Japan where business networking starts with the notorious *keiretsus*. The willingness of many Japanese workers to sacrifice a lot of time and effort in satisfying a customer seems to draw at least partly from the perceived long-term benefits from the alliances created. The Japanese really want to keep a customer at all costs.

COMPLAINTS AS OPPORTUNITIES

In a recent book, Jan Carlzon, the CEO of Scandinavian Airlines System (SAS), discusses the importance of marketing and service at the precise moments when an employee makes contact with the customer.[24] The personal interactions following a company mistake or error are particularly good opportunities to make a good and lasting impression. They are "moments of truth," in Carlzon's phrase. This thinking comes naturally to the Japanese, although their initial response is usually one of complete, catatonic mortification, which initially can be debilitating.

The approach to a complaint is different from that in most Western settings. When a customer complains to a sales clerk in a Western store, the clerk has a problem on her hands. The clerk then typically focuses on solving her own problem, which might be quite opposite that of the customer. For example, by quoting store policies, the clerk denies a request for changed merchandise because the customer did not bring the receipt. The clerk solves her problem, not the customer's.

In Japan, when a customer complains, the sales clerk realizes that the customer has a problem, and then tries to understand exactly what it is. She first empathizes with the customer and adopts the customer's viewpoint to gain a clear understanding of what the customer's problem is. This means listening more than talking, and avoiding judgmental or critical remarks. Exhibit 2:7 spells out some of the more important differences in approach.

Exhibit 2:7
Complaint Handling

United States	Japan
Asking	Listening
Expressing doubt	Expressing sympathy
Explaining what cannot be done	Explaining what can be done
Defending company policy	Apologizing for company policy
Responsibility of the buyer	Responsibility of the seller
"We'll fix it, but..."	"I'm very sorry"
Low customer satisfaction	High customer satisfaction

Although the process is often time-consuming, when the clerk proposes a solution, the customer realizes that the clerk tries to speak to the real issue. This in itself is a source of satisfaction. Furthermore, if no allowance is made because of store policy, the clerk apologizes and expresses sorrow rather than defiance. The customer is made aware very clearly that there is no conflict between the customer and the clerk, while in the West the customer is the "loser." The question of who is right or wrong that permeates the confrontation in the West is avoided at all costs in Japan.[25]

The positive feeling that comes from seeing the clerk trying very hard to fix something is probably not only Japanese but universal. It is a mistake to think that unless the customer gets everything her way she will be dissatisfied. The realization that she has been understood and that somebody has genuinely tried to help is often sufficient to make the customer feel satisfied.

The ready adoption of the customer viewpoint also means that cus-tomers in Japan behave differently. Instead of entering the store with an I-want-my-money-back attitude, which often prohibits a civilized discus-sion of the problem, the Japanese customer is more patient for the clerk to suggest a refund. If you have a problem with service in Japan, you should ask the clerk, "What would you suggest I do?" which is the rele-vant and hard question. In the United States, of course, the clerk's reply might be "What do you want me to do?" or even worse "That's your problem," rather than a fair and customer-focused solution.

TOTAL SATISFACTION

The treatment of the customer as *kamisama* or God has helped the Japanese achieve internationally high levels of customer satisfaction. Their high CS scores derive from a total view of the Japanese company vis-à-vis its customers. High CS scores are not the reward simply from satisfying products and services, but from all interactions and moments of truth with the customer.

All the same, the relationship is still essentially self-serving. The sellers do things for the buyers not from the goodness of their hearts, but for their own gain. The fact that the Japanese sellers firmly claim a long-term view, with motives untainted in the short run, should not hide the fact that their actions to support the buyers are essentially self-serving. About this the Japanese are philosophically sanguine. The clear acceptance of the underlying inequality between the buyer and the seller, and the mutual recognition of the fundamental instrumentality of all interactions, cause the Japanese to avoid direct bargaining. "Don't call attention to marketing," as they fondly say.

In contrast, the American exchange between equals often turns into a crude exercise of quick gains, short-term one-upmanship, and haggling over each transaction. Not a good recipe for customer satisfaction. And as the successful example of GM Saturn's no-hassle sales approach for its autos suggests, even among supposedly cantankerous American buyers there are gains in buyer goodwill and loyalty to be had with a less con-frontational style.

The Japanese have in fact been reengineering for a long time. Lean manufacturing, concurrent engineering, and competitive benchmarking, practices that the West has learned from the Japanese, are only the more well known examples of how companies can become dynamic by doing things better than before. The trick, for the Japanese, is to become more efficient without losing the existing crew of people on board who know the products and the markets. This attitude has important implications for marketing practices, as we will see throughout this book.

It is our firm belief that Western employees would be more than willing to make the necessary sacrifices if only they were matched by sacrifices throughout the company—and if the company could be counted on to provide some job security. People riddled with anxiety who are hounded to perform and uncertain about their prospects with a company are unlikely to provide the kind of customer attention and care that is one of the cornerstones of the Japanese marketing effort. Western companies are likely to pay dearly for their short-sighted layoff strategies and unfair pay scales in the not-so-distant future.

3

MARKET
INFORMATION

Given the preoccupation with the "rational science" side of marketing, marketing research understandably takes a central place among Western marketing tools. The collection of objective market data coupled with quantitative data analysis symbolizes the marketing professional. Progressing from the statistical estimation of demand functions to market share models and psychology-based response models, the well-rounded American "marketeer" must also know such techniques as multidimensional scaling, conjoint analysis, and customer satisfaction measures, and be able to use marketing information systems (MIS) and decision support systems (DSS).[26]

There is, of course, no problem with techniques in and of themselves. Even in the case of the Buick Reatta discussed briefly in chapter 1, the market research filled a necessary function. The fact that the Mazda Miata, as opposed to the Reatta, was a hit without anywhere near the amount of market information backing it up, means simply that numbers are never enough. Intuition and managerial judgment, for all their imperfections, also have to play a role. A few years back, Yankelovich Clancy Shulman, a leading international marketing research and consulting firm, was taken to court by a disgruntled client for projecting market share gains for a new product that were not realized. Yankelovich argued that the marketing support of the launch had been weaker than promised, and the case was settled out of court. Nevertheless, the case underlines the need to bolster quantitative forecasts with managers' intuition of markets and customers. The Japanese marketers are going to great lengths to develop such intuition.

MARKETING RESEARCH

The complexity of advanced marketing research is viewed with suspicion among Japanese marketing nonprofessionals, not simply because of a lack of technical training, but because of a temperamental uneasiness with figuring out people's responses through computerized analyses. Japanese managers' entire upbringing and education have primarily aimed for their socialization into the society and the company, and trying to understand the wishes of other people has become second nature. The basic stimulus-response relationships underlying Western techniques are primitive in comparison to the many possible linkages among different people and actions that they have already learned to discern. People say one thing, do something else. What they say is only an imperfect realization of their feeling. People cannot always explain why they like something. What you hear is not what they said. Western people know this as well, but especially among the multicultural Americans, they have learned to ignore nuances. If it wasn't said, it was not meant. And, since all people need to feel understood, the Americans have learned to be that way, explicit and transparent. So, for the Japanese, it is relatively easy to decipher the American market and figure out the wishes of the customers.[27]

The well-known split in Japanese culture between *honne* and *tatemae* has served the Japanese well in this respect. *Honne* represents the true desires of an individual, while *tatemae* signifies the explicit statement of that desire. What customers say they want might not be what they really want—but for a quantitative analysis, such a distinction is difficult to make. In quantitative analyses the reported responses will usually have to do. For marketers well-versed in reading between the lines, as the Japanese are, the true desires may appear quite obvious without fancy techniques.

For the Japanese marketers, the growth of the advanced marketing research techniques in the United States, so much a part of the professionalization of marketing, has served to distance the company from the customers. The increasing complexity of techniques, meant to track an ever more elusive, affluent, and unpredictable customer, has served mainly to place marketing decisions in the hands of professionals. As in science, numbers speak louder than words. But using more complex techniques is not the answer. Getting closer to the customer is.

VIRTUAL REALITY

How does advanced marketing research complicate the customer-company relationship? In two ways:

• Data collection is done by independent agencies. This means that the input from the customer is limited to predetermined alternatives—the questionnaires often put words in the mouth of the customer. When Western managers listen to the voice of the customer, they are reading responses to questionnaires administered by people they have never met, talking to customers they will never see. Not being there, the managers are unlikely to be able to internalize the responses, to develop tacit knowledge and intuition about the customers.

• The data analysis requires an independent specialist who interprets the responses. The numbers reported in the typical study are computer-generated and based on numerical coding of responses, the raw data. To produce the report, the analyst uses the computer to summarize data, take averages, and calculate various indicators. The customer emerging from such a profile analysis may in fact not exist, in the same way that a short and a tall respondent may erroneously suggest that customers are of average height. The only knowledge gained is that which can be made explicit, at best offering only a starting point for the marketers' imagination. But since the marketers are unlikely to have intuition about the customers anyway, they had better stay away from being too imaginative. It makes Japanese managers think of their own farmers, whose tough work makes it difficult for them to find wives among the new Japanese women: The farmer has to marry a foreigner, choosing from snapshot pictures provided by one of the many marriage agencies.

The potential pitfalls are well-known to most market researchers, and can be hedged against. Nevertheless, once the numbers are in the report and on the table, they tend to take on a life of their own, and cautions are forgotten or ignored. For the Japanese, a better alternative is to listen to the customer's own voice. And the managers themselves should do the listening, as Sam Walton did, not only the market researchers.

To many successful Japanese marketers, the greatest weakness of the questionnaire is that the responses are too far removed from the actual purchase occasion, not that they are intentionally biased or otherwise incorrect. To understand individuals outside the context in which they make their decisions is useless for improving customer satisfaction. The well-known Japanese predilection for situational ethics, whereby a word changes meaning because of the situation and the speaker, means that communications cannot be abstracted from the situation.[28]

When listening to the customer the manager must know the context to fill in missing bits of information and fully understand the customer. When researchers from Kao, Uni-Charm (and now also PandG Japan) interview mothers about desirable features in a disposable diaper, they do it in the home while observing the mother changing the baby. Former U.S. Minolta manager Ned Moro talks about his frequent visits to camera stores to overhear and observe buyers and store clerks exchange information. While in the Western markets a stronger sense of individualism (and democracy) has made the consumers more independent of the social situation and more willing to speak their minds, the sensitivity developed by the Japanese to the context and the unspoken words is still a useful tool for diagnosing customers' real desires. But the listening has to be done in person and on the spot, not through data analysis.

CONSUMER NEEDS AND WANTS

When looking at marketing research practices in Japan, you notice immediately a preoccupation with customer needs. The Japanese have stayed very close to the basics of marketing. The Japanese advertising agencies do a fair amount of testing of advertising messages and promotional campaigns. But because of the frantic pace of new product introductions, most company-sponsored research involves testing customer desires for new features and reactions to new products.

The use of such research is fundamentally to find out more precisely what the customer wants, will need in the future, and would like to have in an existing product. Although the Japanese monitor competitors and test promotional campaigns, they focus on developing new products and features. To the intuitive Japanese minimalist, the interesting consumer behavior question is simply "What kinds of products and services will our customers demand next?" The answer requires a lot of direct observation and talk with users, not advanced scientific methods.

What does "understanding the consumer" mean in American marketing? It goes beyond "wants and needs." Typical discussions of consumer behavior proceed from the hierarchy of needs to the buying process stages and the influence of situational and promotional factors, account for the role of social factors, and proceed to choice strategies and post-purchase feelings. Why do we need to know so much about the individual buyer, and not simply what the buyers want and need in a product or a service?

Marketing research in the West has grown complex and sophisticated and faces more specific management questions. In particular, from the Japanese vantage point, you can see how much of marketing research in the United States obsesses on the management of existing brands in relatively mature markets, partly due to the rise of the brand management concept initiated by Procter & Gamble and copied elsewhere. Quite naturally, in managing brands, the important marketing decisions evolve around relatively short-run promotional efforts, the next advertising campaign, the percentage of shelf space in retail stores, and the unit sales of various package sizes and product forms. While these characteristics have also led some Japanese companies, like Kao, in frequently purchased consumer goods, to adopt Western-style marketing research techniques, the majority of the Japanese companies concentrate on answering the more basic question: What kind of product and service do the customers need?[29] And the Japanese do not think that finding this out is a matter of simply asking them.

You don't ask "What would you like?" in Japan—you always make the effort to provide an alternative: "Perhaps you would like some tea?" You don't say "What do you want in your tea?" but, again, make an effort: "Perhaps you would like some sugar?" The Japanese will never ask a simple "Why?" as in "Why did you choose that?" because it is a crude, slack-minded, and confrontational question. They will perhaps offer a plausible explanation, even attribute it to themselves: "I like this tea's flavor." In most cases, the "why" is immaterial as a question anyway; the Japanese do not expect a true answer, or even any answer. Perhaps as a consequence (it is hard to say which came first), many Japanese cannot answer the "why" in precise terms, which, in turn, has led them to reject Western logic, sometimes at their own peril. The Japanese are thoroughly postmodern in their thinking, not expecting human actions to be based on carefully thought-out reasoning. But this is now, of course, also a strong current in Western thinking, as in Henry Mintzberg's 1994 book, *The Rise and Fall of Strategic Planning*, which is a clarion call for the role of intuition in business.[30]

CONSUMER RESPONSE

A large part of the study of consumer behavior in the United States focuses on the responses of individuals to the buying stimuli offered by new product features, special services, and alternative advertising messages. Marketing research as a field of inquiry is not satisfied to predict acceptance of new products and to detect the trends emerging in the marketplace, but tries to explain and predict consumer responses to various instruments of persuasion. According to its practitioners, such study is not intrinsically manipulative, since it is only in the use of the findings that manipulation might occur.

The better defense against manipulative charges, if one is needed, would perhaps be to argue that the use of constraining scientific methodologies in the field of consumer behavior have meant that the external relevance of the findings is limited. This is basically the Japanese reaction to much of consumer behavior research in the United States. The "real" consumer cannot be gleaned from questionnaire responses or simulated lab tests, but only in actual product use. Honda calls this the *sangen* or "three actuals" approach, with three requirements: actual product, actual person, actual situation.[31]

Honda places great importance on learning about a market firsthand, and has confidence in the ability of its people to learn about the market and its customers directly. Designers and marketers avoid making assumptions about the market and the customers, believing that in this way they can get closer to the market. They evaluate the information themselves and try to look at all the facts. The guiding principles in data analysis are (1) all facts are necessary, and (2) not all the facts are quantifiable. Following the *sangen* dictum, the company has assigned a number of its engineers and designers to marketing research functions in overseas market locations. For example, Honda's research and development unit in Irvine, California, includes engineers who attempt to infer future car needs in the United States on the basis of Californian consumer styles and habits.

For example, in the parking lot at Disneyland Honda's designers observed how drivers and passengers entered and exited cars, which led to wider front doors and seats closer to the door so that women with skirts could more easily get into the driver's seat. The way users opened the trunk suggested the sweep of the lid and the required angle for the hatchback door in the up position. Noticing how people had to lift things up from the trunk, the designers decided to make trunks without sills for easy sliding. Realizing that American drivers swung their elbows wider than Japanese drivers led designers to a hollowed-out door design made possible with stronger steel alloys. Such hands-on research exemplifies Honda's dictum: "Man maximum, machine minimum."

Assessment of consumer response to existing models is naturally done by most Japanese companies via their middlemen and by talking to customers. Matsushita representatives make a point of visiting stores to observe interactions between customers and store clerks, talk to salespeople and customers, and troubleshoot in-store factors, such as lack of product information and poor displays. Toyota teams of engineers, planners, researchers, and marketers, as well as Japanese executives, visit dealers and travel to diverse markets to talk to customers. These teams spend most of their time talking to the dealership's service manager, technicians, salespeople, and customers, not the dealer principal. The intent is to ask about what sorts of problems they are experiencing with Toyota products, and how they feel Toyota could improve, not to hear how great Toyota cars are.

MASS CUSTOMIZATION

Close relationships and active interactions with customers are today very important to all corporations. Recent dramatic developments in information technologies have allowed corporations easy, cost-efficient access to individual consumers. Corporations are now able to provide products and services that fully cater to the needs of each individual consumer: "mass customization." As the economy becomes more mature and sophisticated, however, consumers frequently have a difficult time expressing their own needs specifically. It is particularly difficult for them to explain what makes for abstract values such as *beauty* and *pleasing*. Today's corporations are requested to understand the tacit sense of consumers in order to develop new products that truly cater to their needs.

One of the pioneers in one-to-one marketing was the National Bicycle Manufacturing Company, Ltd., a subsidiary of Matsushita, which started customized bicycle manufacturing in 1986. In November of that year, Mitsuru Omoto assumed his new post as president of the company. Until then, Omoto's career had nothing to do with bicycles. An experienced consumer electronics manager, he was suddenly given the challenge of making a new breakthrough in the stagnant bicycle industry.

Because the demand for ordinary sport bicycles for average users was decreasing, Omoto turned his attention to the increasing demand for customized sport bicycles for serious users, a niche resulting from diversified consumer needs and the fitness boom. Omoto decided to introduce computer systems into the company's production system so that each product was made to order. To make the system profitable, he also aimed to reduce production costs and cut the order-to-delivery cycle. There has always been a dilemma in the customized production of bicycles for serious users because of the low profit in craftsmanship-oriented production by skilled workers. Omoto wanted to overcome this dilemma by incorporating computer systems into the company's customized-production system. Such a new manufacturing/distribution system would not only open a market but also clearly differentiate the company from its competitors.

Accurate measurement was a critical factor for the success of the Panasonic Ordering System, or POS. In the beginning, everyone though it would be extremely difficult to measure each customer while in motion. But the company decided that they could not make a bicycle truly fitted to each user unless they measured the user while he or she was actually on a bicycle. Since any such tacit knowledge is specific to the riding experience, one should not think it can be easily translated into explicitly verbal knowledge.

The POS system required a method that tapped into each customer's preferences and measured the size of his or her body. The company developed a tool to help customers describe when they felt comfortable on bicycles. The tool, called a fitting scale, looked very much like a bicycle without wheels. A POS customer was asked to sit on the fitting scale while legs, reach, and shoulder width were accurately measured. A staff member of the POS store identified the most comfortable riding position for the customer by adjusting the scale of the bike mock-up.

There are today more than one thousand POS agent stores throughout Japan. Each of them is equipped with a fitting scale and color samples. First the customer is measured against the fitting scale. Then the customer chooses a color pattern for his or her bicycle from several colors available. Combinations of these colors allow for a number of color patterns. The customer also chooses logos to be printed on the bicycle's top bar or frame. Orders for POS bicycles are faxed directly to the factory, and bicycles are built in a very short period: two weeks. The data on the order form is entered in the factory's CAM host computer, and a UPC bar code representing the same data is generated and sent to the production line. During the production procedure, which begins with the process of building the frame, everything is done as specified by the code until the delivery of the finished product. The order form is then sent to the sales administration and circulated to a sales company or an agent and the retailer to collect the bill.

Mass customization represents a logical extension of being close to the (individual) customer and doing hands-on research. Western industries are now starting to realize the benefits of flexible manufacturing and one-to-one marketing, including shoes and apparel.[32]

HANDS-ON TECHNIQUES

Even hands-on marketing research requires skill. Since managers carry out this research, they need to develop these skills to some acceptable level.

Good hands-on marketing research requires first of all sensitivity to the customer's situation, an empathy that makes it possible to put oneself into the other person's place. You have to know how to ask (and how not to ask) good questions, and how to be a sympathetic and active listener. All these qualities tend to be nursed at home and in school in Japan, in contrast to what is happening in the United States. Nevertheless, since the Japanese cannot use these skills to the fullest in the West because of the language problems, not all is lost for the less skillful Westerner.

The key lies in seeing what is going on. Hands-on research in marketing involves, above all, observation of customers' behavior. And listening to the consumers involves a lot of watching their behavior, in-store and using the product. This the Japanese do very well.

Early examples include Toyota's use of the VW Beetle for test drives to decide which features to imitate and which to improve; and the molding of cup holders on dashboards after Toyota's engineers saw Los Angeles drivers balancing coffee cups while driving on the freeway. More recent examples include the redesign of Sony's Walkman to withstand accidental drops, the most frequent cause of malfunctioning; the drive from Brussels to Milano by a Nissan design team to develop ideas for the design of their "European" car, the Primera; and the sure-shot handle created by Canon for its new automatic cameras to enable picture taking with one hand.

Nintendo, the manufacturer of electronic games, has had a virtual stranglehold on its market for the last decade, and did no market research until Sega, another Japanese company, challenged it. Still, both companies are more concerned with technology, and treat their market research as secondary to product research. But the new products are developed with the help of users. Young children are asked to participate in the test centers set up in Tokyo and Osaka where new products are first introduced by the companies.

These kinds of product design features do not emerge easily from the typical questionnaires used for Western-style market research. In fact, they are unlikely to emerge from professional marketers' or designers' observations of customers, since their training makes them miss seemingly trivial facts such as how people stand, walk, or move their arms when they use a product.[33] Attention to such obvious behaviors underlies much of the so-called Taguchi school of quality control. The Taguchi method springs from a philosophy that attempts to design the product around the user rather than imposing itself on the user. Although in many cases the result comes close to Western-style functionalism, the thinking goes deeper. While functionalism attempts to maximize the product performance through design, the Taguchi method starts with the user and tries to maximize user performance. This is a natural, but almost revolutionary, perspective that helps explain why nonprofessional Japanese marketers "seem to have gotten the American consumer's number," to quote Jack Welch.

Most electronic products, such as the early stereos, required a sequence of steps for turning off and on. Observing users, the Japanese manufacturers soon realized that consumers would prefer one-button operations, with an option to do more as needed. This observation led to the automatic startup of a VCR tape as it is inserted, the possibility of ejecting the tape without turning on the power, and the stopping of play by simply turning the power off. In these and similar examples the Taguchi-style philosophy produces design results strikingly different from the product-oriented approaches of engineering powers in the West, such as Germany.[34]

According to the Japanese, for this kind of user observation, the more innocence or "white mind" the observer possesses, the better. This is why they generally prefer to send new people abroad rather than seasoned veterans. While people who have lived a few years in a foreign country will know how to take care of things, they will also be less sensitive to the peculiarities of people's behavior. How carefully people handle products will determine how sturdy a design has to be; how they sit when they use the product will determine the amount of space required; how loudly they speak will determine the required volume capacity; how much attention they pay to instructions determines what the level of assembly tasks can be; and so on. While many of these requirements come naturally to designers in the country, some are also ignored precisely because they are too "natural" to be observable. In fact, the Western tolerance of deviant actions often means that observers consciously or unconsciously ignore differences in behavior. Here the very insularity of the Japanese coupled with their reluctance to impose their norms on others have helped them design more "friendly" products. The Japanese have developed and sustained competitive advantages on such seemingly thin bases.

AN ILLUSTRATION

Examples of hands-on research are particularly common for entry into new foreign markets. The experiences of managers at Toyota and Honda in the late 1950s in the California market have been well-documented elsewhere.[35] It is striking to find such a relatively haphazard, intuitive type of market approach as late as the mid-seventies. The following case is a description of how Canon, the big camera company, established its own distribution in the U.S. market.[36]

Canon's cameras had been sold in the United States since the 1950s, and from 1963 Bell & Howell, an American company, had served as sole distributor for the United States. In 1972 Canon decided to establish a direct sales organization to increase control over marketing and attempt to raise its market share. Tatehiro Tsuruta, the new head of Canon

America, went to the United States as a leader of a three-member team.

He remembers: "I had never dreamed of going abroad, having spent all my previous life in corporate planning. The other two team members had the same lack of experience.

"None of us knew much about the market in the U.S. The head of exporting at HQ in Japan and all the others at home had no idea of what could be accomplished. They were amateurs as us when it came to American business—or any overseas business, for that matter.

"The United States was a big country, with few houses, and even though New York was crowded, once you got out of the city you saw no people. We would talk into the night at our hotel about what kind of marketing to do in such a place.

"I did some market research by walking around to the camera stores in Manhattan to see whether the Canon products were available in the shops. There were not so many—and the same was true of Chicago. I realized right away that Canon's prices were very high and that Canon cameras were not very competitive with other Japanese makes. I later found out that this was because B&H objectives centered on profits—and if the cameras did not offer enough of a margin, prices were simply increased until a target rate was reached.

"I also found out by talking to the dealers that the B&H salesmen had an arrogant attitude toward the retailers, and essentially took a take-it-or-forget-it approach to selling them Canons. The retailers did not like them, naturally. They told me they wanted to deal with Canon but not through B&H.

"The Japanese and European markets differed from the U.S. considerably. In the latter market, I was told by the dealers, the customers considered an SLR camera at about $300 for professionals and advanced amateurs, whereas in Europe and Japan these cameras, although actually as expensive—if not more—were the only ones considered worthwhile."

As with all hands-on research, the quality of this type of market information depends directly on the experience and knowledge—and an adjustment for the likely biases—of the dealers contacted. In this regard, American specialty camera dealers seem to have been very astute, considering Canon's later market success.

IMPLEMENTING FINDINGS

One test of a good company is whether it will act on the information collected. The Japanese companies are very aware of the ease with which even the best ideas get lost and pay close attention to implementing suggestions. They use hands-on market research not only for short-term fixes, but try to get to the root of problems. When Honda's dealer research found that one of their car models exhibited wobbly steering at speeds in excess of ninety miles per hour, the engineers got to work. Within less than two months a complex but flawed steering column sub-assembly had been corrected, and within four months the new design was implemented and introduced even before the new model year. There had been no direct customer complaints, since ninety miles per hour is above the typical speed limits. (This 1989 incident foreshadows Intel's rather different approach to the Pentium chip problem.)

The Japanese attention to product functioning and service support is born out of good business sense and not smart psychology. Offering the best quality possible is simply good business, and in this sense the Japanese are "manipulating" the Western consumers. The point is, as we saw in chapter 2, that this type of manipulation is intrinsically part of the buyer-seller relationship, and thus needs no excuse or expression.

A consequence of the Japanese attention to basic needs and overt behavior among their own homogeneous population is a quite stereotypical notion of individual consumers. Japanese buyers are seen as fickle because there are many comparable manufacturers. The tendency of the Japanese to "lead" market preferences with new products and engage in "destruction" of their own market leader brands flows from the same simple view of buyer psychology. In turn this means that companies' marketing efforts react strongly to small shifts in competitor behavior, something criticized by Japanese observers.[37]

Because companies cannot easily predict such things as the consumer acceptance of a new product, Western companies resort to complex consumer behavior models and sophisticated analytical techniques. The solution for leading Japanese companies is to do a full-court press, have designers, engineers, salespeople, and managers all in direct contact with customers, talk to them about what they like and don't like about old products and new test products, try to improve on it, listen actively and creatively to what they might want in the future, present the new variant to the market, and hope. When they fail, instead of resorting to pushy promotional strategies to convince the consumers of the advantages of the new variants or products, they quickly regroup and try again. Hamel and Prahalad have termed this expeditionary marketing.[38] Despite its inelegance and seeming waste, it works in the kinds of market situations in which the Japanese find themselves, with high consumer knowledge coupled with complex products. In mature markets for durable consumer products, their product orientation and customer orientation are intimately connected.

HARD AND SOFT DATA

The Japanese marketers pay a lot of attention to what one might call "hard" market data. These are quantifiable figures on warehouse shipments, in-store turnover figures, competitive prices, and derived market share figures broken down by brand, product form, and package size, by outlet, and by customer group where possible. The figures are collected as frequently as possible, in some extreme cases daily (such as Kao's figures for shipments from its wholly owned distributorships). Generally the frequency is higher than in the West, since the manufacturers' control over distribution in Japan is typically greater.

Such hard data are used to construct inventory control diagrams, turnover charts, and tables of market share movements, practices that owe much to the statistical instinct inculcated by the Deming quality teaching.[39] In the case of 7-Eleven stores, owned by the superstore chain of Ito-Yokado, computerized product and customer data are used to help store managers forecast buying behavior on a daily and weekly basis. Central planning and inventory control are inefficient because of local variations—festivals, weather, sporting events—in daily demand. Ito-Yokado's system allows local managers to order quantities and product selections that fit their local demand variations—and check orders against forecasts on computer terminals in each store. But the Japanese marketers as a rule rely much less on the computerized data analyses concerning customer perceptions, attitudes, and behavioral intentions common in the West. Instead the managers themselves take time out to visit stores, talk to dealers, listen to customers, and observe consumers—hands-on market research. They want to be informed on a firsthand basis, to "smell" the marketplace, to understand the context in which the buying and selling take place. It is the marketing equivalent of the management-by-walking-around approach.

The associated tendency to rely on informal "analysis" and subjective interpretation of customer responses is strengthened by the fact that the Japanese home market is peculiarly homogeneous. A common education, uniform mass media, and relative isolation from the rest of the world have combined to make the preferences of the Japanese consumers strikingly similar. Add a desire not to stray too far from the group norms, and buying behavior in mature markets in Japan is not so difficult to predict. But new trends—and Japanese markets have more than their share of new trends because of the strong economic growth—are difficult to predict, and new product failures are common, according to company insiders. However, once the direction is clear, most of the companies try to get on the bandwagon in their imitative fashion. Thus, hands-on research means keeping one's ear to the ground at all times, not to miss out on the next development.

In larger and less homogeneous markets, such as the United States, the intuitive market researcher has perhaps less chance to be right. Subjective interpretation of a few customer responses are too unreliable when customers and analysts come from widely different subcultures, and when the population is heterogeneous. Large-scale surveys are preferable in such cases, and many successful Japanese companies that may not use formal marketing research at home will use it abroad.

But even in foreign markets, their tendency to imitate successful competitors' products has meant that the reliance on in-depth systematic analysis has been less than that of the Western companies. In the United States, in particular, the explicit and low-context culture has helped the Japanese companies understand buyer motivation well. The strategy of intuitive incrementalism, discussed in the next chapter, has also helped, since every step is viewed as another test of market reaction, and new learning is digested and applied cumulatively over time. Add to that the fact that the United States has been the big target market for the Japanese ever since World War II—for some companies, such as Honda and Sony, the U.S. market is even bigger than the home market—and the notion that the Japanese products are designed as if the Japanese can read the customers' minds has a natural growing ground.

ENVIRONMENTAL SCANNING

The downplaying of formal marketing research by the Japanese does not mean that they act without being informed. As many observers of business negotiations have pointed out, the Japanese tend to be better prepared and have greater access to information than their Western counterparts. Similarly, in their marketing endeavors, the Japanese tend to be more fully informed than many Western competitors.[40] How is this?

INFORMATION JUNKIES

The Japanese read voraciously from early years on, and their education places great value on book knowledge. Before they take any action, the Japanese would like to minimize the downside risks, and thus collect all possibly relevant information. They have been called information "junkies."[41] When they are uncertain, they hesitate, and would rather wait until more information is available.

What the Japanese do not do is to create *a priori* theories about the behavior of markets that would delimit their information search. While Western marketing professionals are prone to develop narrowly focused explanations for the behavior of consumers and competitors, and then test these theories against quantitative data collected for the specific purpose, the Japanese are content simply to sift through data, run simple summary analyses of trends and averages, but also look at a much wider set of data. Information overload seems not to exist for the Japanese.

When a Japanese employee at a Western subsidiary in Tokyo was asked to keep an eye on relevant industry developments in the daily press, he spent all day reading the newspapers and translating articles. "It is all relevant," he explained to the astonished boss.[42] In Japanese subsidiaries in the West some employees do in fact spend a lot of their day scanning Western newspapers and faxing "relevant" articles back home to Tokyo headquarters. Typical is the following remark made by a Japanese executive from Sharp Electronics in response to a question about how his company finds out about the American consumer: "We do everything. We use syndicated data, surveys, focus groups. For example, we subscribe to a 'trendsetter' study which tracks lifestyles and buying patterns in thirty to forty states in order to monitor changes. We also travel to dealers, stores, ask customers what they like, and so on." Nissan's debacle of placing a student "informant" with a California host family to gather data on American family life is an extreme example of the length to which companies will go to gather market information.

This 1986 incident, which was highly publicized at the time—featured on the front business page of the *New York Times*—caught the Japanese company by surprise. The story has a background. Since lifetime employment and job rotation are still common in Japanese companies, a young company employee with an undergraduate college degree, after a few years on the job, will often get a chance to go to graduate school abroad to obtain a master's degree, often an MBA. As a consequence, many Japanese students at universities in the West are sponsored by companies, and expect to return there afterward. Via fax and telephone they often maintain close contact with the company back home, if for no other reason than to keep track of colleagues' promotions and other career-affecting events. Quite naturally, the companies come to see these students as a source of information about the country in which they study, and the students can make a mark for themselves by breaking the news about some development of importance to the company.

Even though these Japanese students' major aim is typically to get acculturated in the foreign country and develop potentially useful contacts with fellow students, they also have to do some studying. The "environmental scanning" function necessarily takes a backseat to other concerns. But Nissan recognized the value of a student affiliation as a legitimizing role for intelligence gathering. The company sent an employee to enroll in a college in Los Angeles, and also instructed him to stay with an American host family rather than in a school dormitory. This "undercover" student proceeded to observe and record the host family's shopping and consumption behavior, making periodic reports to the company. Ultimately the American family discovered the "spying," reacted angrily, and sued the student and the company. To avoid damage, the case was settled out of court by embarrassed Nissan executives without admission of wrongdoing.

An interesting aspect of this story from a Western perspective is, of course, what the company thought it was getting from the information. An average American family's lifestyle in California may be interesting, but their home is unlikely to house any hidden Myst secrets. But from the Japanese perspective, even finding out that Californians back their car out of the garage with a "thump" on the pavement, or slam down the telephone hard on the hook is information—as is, of course, the insight that Californians try to drink hot coffee while driving, a finding that has made millions for them.

IMPORTANT INFORMATION?

How does a marketer decide when market information is important? Any data collection effort requires a certain theory about what data are useful and at least implicit calculation of the costs of collecting information and its economic benefits. In marketing, sales figures, market shares, new product introduction rates, store movement, and so on are usually viewed as key indicators of performance for an ongoing enterprise and worth the costs involved in tracking them over time.

However, the benefits from such data are directly proportional to the rate of, and vulnerability to, change in the marketplace. How fast do customer preferences change, and are new competitive offerings introduced? Do new distribution channels and advertising campaigns challenge our position? To the extent the individual firm can isolate itself from such changes, through entry barriers such as niche segmentation, tariffs, patent protection, and so on, the need for information gathering lessens. In cases in which a clear niche is targeted, or in which a technological barrier exists, or in which long-term investments have raised the transaction costs for new entrants, the incentive for information gathering will be lower. Artificial barriers, such as trade restrictions, or natural barriers, such as brand-loyal customers, lessen the need for information. Marketing, whether by a Western company or a Japanese company, is largely a matter of building protection for one's brands and attempting to smash the defenses of competitors' brands. But while a Western brand traditionally attempted to do this by building on its uniqueness, creating and protecting sustainable advantages, the Japanese have less of a chance to do this.

Among Western firms, marketers are trained to aim for differentiation, the creation of unique products or services that offer some sustainable competitive advantage and an opportunity for above-normal profits. This is in contrast to many of the Japanese companies, which see little possibility of being unique vis-à-vis their Japanese rivals.

The Japanese do not have assets in the land itself in the way companies in the resource-rich countries of the West tend to have. Unequal access to natural resources differentiates between firms in the West. Not in Japan. The possession of technological patents and know-how differentiates products in the West. Less so in Japan. Japanese firms rely on people as their most important distinguishing resource. If one company can differentiate itself from another, it is because of its people and their achievements, not because of differences in underlying endowments. Any advantage is precarious, and monitoring of competitors' activities and customer preferences comes as natural and is as inevitable as eating and drinking. Information is the lifeblood of the Japanese "traders."

US VERSUS THEM

In foreign marketplaces, Japanese subsidiaries value general information more highly than do Western marketers, partly because of their geographic location, but also because of their insistence that they differ dramatically from other people. As a result they feel alien in foreign cultures, and Japanese managers often emphasize their lack of understanding of customs in Western countries. By contrast, many North American and European countries have a long history of interchange with foreign nations, and many Western businessmen feel quite at home in many countries. The uncertainties of doing business in general in the West will be greater for a Japanese company than for a Western firm. If the monetary stakes and the attitudes to risk are roughly similar, it is not surprising to find the Japanese subsidiaries in the West collecting more information for this reason alone.[43]

In recent years the wide Japanese information gathering abroad has been further stimulated because the Japanese face not only the typical business risks but increasing political pressure and potential government interference. To survive they have to scan for new developments of trade policy, protectionist threats, exchange rate manipulations, and related changes in the world's economies and trade regimes. The Japanese information-gathering activities are so widespread and intensive partly because they cannot afford to be caught off-guard by any developments.

Apart from its own global network, the large Japanese company—as well as the small one—can access information provided by external sources: the government agencies—Jetro offices, consulates, and various ministries' representatives abroad—the local Japanese chambers of commerce, and, of course, the trading company networks. As of 1995, the largest, Itohchu, maintained offices in ninety countries, bought and sold an estimated thirty thousand products, and collected information on any political or economic development that might be of some business value.[44]

ANALYSIS IN-HOUSE

How are such data digested and transmitted to the right people in the organization, especially headquarters back home? As more data are collected the information easily overloads organizational channel capacities, no?

Compared to Western companies, Japanese companies have more people assigned to information-gathering activities. In foreign subsidiaries as well as headquarters more people are assigned to assimilate the data transmitted. It is not unusual, for example, for several junior managers to receive, analyze, and diffuse market information from abroad. Although costly, it has advantages. It increases processing capacity and helps avoid information overload. The redundancy increases reliability of the data, since individual misreadings are spotted and quickly corrected. Also, it allows a dialogue-type analysis by which different perspectives are brought to bear on seemingly contradictory evidence, and the big picture synthesized more quickly. Finally, data analysis can be done at headquarters by company analysts. Many Japanese companies overseas ask market research providers to transmit data to headquarters for the company to do its own analysis. It keeps costs down, avoids overreliance on foreign research analysts, and allows headquarters to develop a much better sense for the local market.

In most Western companies where the local subsidiaries are profit centers, the market research reports to headquarters are likely to be much more narrowly focused on market tracking and sales analyses. The field offices will only report summary figures and results of analyses to headquarters, in effect shielding the home office from the local market. It is also possible that the market information is biased, whether intentionally or not. In both the local subsidiary and at headquarters, few employees are assigned the research tasks. If one employee cannot handle the load, the solution is likely to be one by which the load is divided up among several individuals, usually with help from outside consultants or hired experts. Again, it introduces a filter between the market and the firm, and, in the name of efficiency, forgoes the desirable reliability effect of redundancy.[45]

COMPETING ON TIME

The frequency and speed of information gathering depends naturally upon the perceived urgency of the firm's situation, a matter of the pace of environmental change and competitive rivalry. Overseas, where many Japanese companies are attacked by other Japanese entrants, they track markets closely and try to respond quickly to new challenges.

Partly because of their lack of uniqueness, the Japanese companies usually face intense competition from compatriots in their markets. Typically when one Japanese company has entered a new market, so can (and will) one or more of its competitors from Japan. It started with East Asia, then Australia, then the United States, and now China.[46] Thus, the competitive situation often forces price reductions and lower profits on existing products. One result has been to speed up the new product introductions, driving the market to new highs. As one company does this, others follow with improvements of their own. To neutralize the competitive effect, the firm needs to monitor its competitors continuously, and make sure that any first-mover advantage is short-lived. Information about technological developments, competitive innovations, and new products is gathered and digested quickly, and countermoves are designed. Kyocera, the Kyoto-based high-technology company with a dominant share of the world's market for ceramic housing for electronic chips, gives its salespeople a salary-plus-bonus pay scheme, and no commissions, to encourage their market and competitive scanning efforts.[47]

Access to rapid information recovery also feeds back to quicker responses and competitive countermoves, and thus speeds up the dynamics of the marketplace. In turn, competing companies must collect and disseminate timely data, and react quickly. If Japanese companies react faster, they will force non-Japanese companies to also speed up their processing. Competing on time requires timely information analyzed quickly. When the Japanese enter new countries and markets (in mature markets where change has been slow), their entry speeds up changes and creates a more dynamic competitive situation. The Japanese way with information comes to dominate less intensive efforts, and forces Western companies to speed up.[48]

GLOBAL NETWORKS

The broad coverage of data collection in Japanese corporations ties directly to the role for local field offices and foreign subsidiaries in the global network. Japanese subsidiaries in various countries assist one another with information gathering as the need arises, and alert one another to business risks and opportunities. Fuji film's successful bid to sponsor the 1984 Summer Olympics in Los Angeles is a case in point. It was triggered by an employee in Fuji's London office. Hearing from a British source close to Kodak that the company was balking at the steep price quoted by Peter Ueberroth, the head of the organizing committee, he immediately faxed the U.S. office of Fuji in New Jersey.[49] Such direct contacts are made easier by the policy of lifetime employment, with everybody belonging to the company "family," and the hiring at entry levels only (so that a new expatriate manager in New York is likely to have a friend of about the same age in the office in Zurich, for example).

Expatriate Japanese talk of their subsidiary as a member of a global network. "Networking," "cross-subsidization," and "cross-fertilization" are terms typically used, now also in the West. Yes, sooner or later local subsidiaries must carry their own weight by showing profitable operations. But the network benefits of the subsidiary accrue to the system whether or not profits are made. By sharing information about new technological developments, about competitive entries, and about the foreign environment in general, a subsidiary creates benefits elsewhere in the network. It is not "tight coupling" between units, using transfer prices and allocation of resources algorithms, but a still tangible "organizational learning and sharing" process understood and accepted by all company members.

The Japanese abroad communicate frequently with the home office, usually via telephone or fax. When face-to-face communication is necessary, the Japanese at headquarters travel to the subsidiary, to understand the situation better and to avoid disrupting local operations. For them it makes little sense to discuss a foreign market back in Tokyo, where the context of the problems would be less fully understood—the *sangen* principle again. This policy is facilitated by the fact that there are usually enough people at headquarters to take care of issues there even with managers absent. On the downside, it means that Japanese expatriates must run the overseas subsidiaries.

A RESOURCE VIEW

The Japanese have increasingly come to view information as a key resource in the future global world. Of course, everybody seems to think that we are moving toward an "information society," but nowhere is the emphasis upon the emerging information and communication sciences stronger than in Japan. One reason is undoubtedly that such a future would not put a premium on raw material–based heavy industries but rather on high-tech industries and their associated need for educated people. It goes well with the notion that people are the only differentiating resource giving the firm a competitive advantage.

This underlying perspective helps explain why the Japanese are so willing to cast a broad net of information coverage. To focus only on the present industry and market is folly, and places the future of the company at risk. It is not that diversification is the intended strategy. But technology and innovations from other markets and industries may affect developments in the company's industry. Furthermore, since Japan is not the only place where new technological, social, and economic trends emanate, foreign subsidiary management would not fulfill its duties simply by looking at the present product markets. To develop a global network, avoid treating the subsidiaries as freestanding profit centers.

The Western profit-seeking subsidiary simply cannot afford to ignore the bottom-line concerns to the same extent. After a reasonably long startup period, both headquarters and subsidiary management expect to make money. Even in the absence of strong pressure from the home office, no Western subsidiary manager would hesitate to cut out some labor-intensive broad-scale monitoring of the American environment if the time to show positive returns had come.

While marketing research may not be as sophisticated in Japan as in the West, the environmental scanning ability and the amount of information about the firm's larger environment easily rivals that of the best Western companies. Fueled by a strong and insistent sense of insecurity about the future at home and abroad, the Japanese seem never to think that they now know the market sufficiently to satisfy their appetite for more information.

The role of people in the field must be fundamentally reevaluated. In typical theories of organizational learning, the business environment is treated simply as the source of stimulation and information, while people who interface with such environments–that is, those who work for the sales and marketing sectors–are treated as "sense organs" whose role is just to convey outside stimuli to the information-processing division, the corporation's brain. But employees in the field accumulate ample tacit knowledge through their everyday interactions with customers. Middle managers, the leaders of the front-line personnel, must not only cultivate their sensitivity but also help them develop an ability to translate the knowledge gained in daily practice and utilize it organizationally. In short, the salespeople must not be simple sensing or conveying devices but the front line of new knowledge creation. Managers at the front line must play the role of knowledge engineers, who facilitate the knowledge accumulation through direct interactions with customers and others and transform the knowledge of their staff members and customers into effective concepts for the organization.

➤ PART II
INTUITIVE STRATEGISTS

4
TRIAL AND
ERROR

Strategic market planning in the West involves a considerable amount of premeditation and technical analysis. In the standard Western-style analysis, companies first match their strengths and weaknesses against opportunities and threats in the market environment to formulate a fitting strategy. They then implement the strategy by mixing the competitive advantages of the firm into an optimal marketing program that positions the product in the preselected target segment.[50]

A good example of the Western approach is the launch of the Ford Mustang in 1964. This was one of the first applications of the product positioning concept, which tests the product concept against target segment preferences; fine-tunes features, design, and style; and, where promotion emphasizes the uniqueness of the new product, distinguishes it clearly from competitors in the marketplace. The point is to find a place in the product space and mind of the customer that you can "own."

Mindful of its recent Edsel debacle, the Ford marketers led by a young Lee Iacocca initiated the Mustang project only after many previous Mustang owners had expressed a desire to see a new sports car from Ford. The first Mustang, a sleek and relatively expensive sports car from the mid-1950s, had been discontinued a few years earlier after sales had slowed. From market research the project team recognized that the new car had to be lower-priced, but still have a sporty image. From the research the team developed a positioning theme of youth and fun, styled the car similarly to the original, used a basic Ford chassis and engine to reduce costs, and expanded the seating capacity from two to the slightly more accommodating two-plus-two, allowing the advertising to feature groups of young kids riding together to the beach for fun and games.

The result was one of the great success stories of American marketing. Acceptance was immediate, sales soared, and competition was left behind (even though GM tried to counter with the rear-engined Corvair). Ford executives traveled the lecture circuit to business schools explaining how the new methods worked. But, as they somewhat sheepishly admitted, the target market had been misjudged. Instead of young adults, the typical Ford Mustang buyers were middle-aged males, reminiscing nostalgically about lost youth, and making enough money in the upbeat sixties to be able to indulge in their dreams.

Not to worry. Product positioning, for all its problems, was better than what had been there before. Some positioning research would undoubtedly have helped the early Japanese pioneers into the American market. In the early 1960s Honda thought only big motorbikes had potential in the United States, but found out that its smaller bikes were better bets. The sustained highway driving in California broke the oil seals of Honda's 250cc bikes, and they had to be redesigned back in Japan. Meanwhile, Honda's representatives in Los Angeles traveled on their little 50cc Supercubs, sleeker than the outmoded mopeds of the day, which caught the eye of a Sears buyer. His offer to sell the bikes under the Sears name was refused, but Honda managers realized that their small bikes might be successful. Supported by the now-classic advertising slogan, "You meet the nicest people on a Honda," developed by a UCLA student, sales of the small bikes took off, creating a whole new market for motorbikes in the United States.

Toyota's Toyopet, the largest car built by Toyota at the end of the 1950s, was naturally the one used to spearhead Toyota's entry into the U.S. market. But as in the case of Honda, the Toyopet was just not sturdy enough for the California highways—and, again, the better niche in the market was for a smaller car, the Corona, which competed successfully with the VW Beetle. Having learned its lesson, Toyota never looked back, introducing the Corolla, the Celica, and the Cressida as it gradually increased market share over the next few years.[51]

While Western marketers pursued the development of the scientific side of marketing, the Japanese have continued for their part to rely more on a trial-and-error strategy. Of course, Japanese companies like Sony, Matsushita, and YKK, the world-leading zipper maker, are known for long-range planning, including grand schemes for the future of their organizations and their country. Japanese companies use advanced planning tools in manufacturing, especially for operations scheduling. In marketing, however, the Japanese tend to be less "strategic" and less technical than Western businesses. In foreign markets in particular, where they face a great deal of uncertainty, they shun grand schemes and formal planning techniques. Rather, they rely on trial-and-error, learning gradually from small steps, and constantly adjusting decisions and objectives. They are what you might call "intuitive incrementalists."

Intuitive Incrementalism

Whereas strategic planning in the West typically cascades down in logical steps from broad mission statements to more specific objectives to the enumeration of tasks, the assignment of responsibilities, and the fixing of a time schedule, the Japanese approach is fuzzier. The intuitive incrementalism of the Japanese means essentially experience-based learning, a natural or "organic" process. It involves a lot of initial information sharing, agreeing to do something relatively small, getting quick feedback, pondering it, and discussing it, then doing something small again.[52] The early information sharing allows everyone affected to learn about what is coming; the first step simply represents a commitment to do something to get things started.

INNOCENTS ABROAD

Why would the Japanese rather get something going than do a more thorough analysis? One reason is that, as we saw in the previous chapter, the Japanese believe that true understanding comes from direct exposure to the customers and competitors in the market. The companies avoid hard calculations or pros and cons when the data are uncertain—as nonprofessionals they don't believe that they should treat complex marketing questions as engineering problems. They base their commitment to a course of action less on a logical derivation from broader objectives, and more on an intuitive connection between what the company "must do" or "stand for" and what the necessary marketing actions will be.[53] And after their improbable and miraculous comeback after World War II, they are genuinely afraid of developing "paralysis through analysis."

The way the Japanese approach market entries abroad illustrates their general approach to strategic planning. The Honda and Toyota stories represent only the tip of the iceberg.[54] The pioneers sent over were all basically new to the country. Even today, many Japanese companies prefer to send to America Japanese managers who have never been there, ostensibly to preserve a certain "freshness" in their outlook on the market, as if the Japanese feared being "too expert" in marketing. Such a practice also helps in exercising control of the enterprise from Japan, since the neophyte becomes more dependent on headquarters for advice.

Perhaps not so surprisingly, to gain insights into the new markets, these "innocents abroad" talk directly to wholesalers, retailers, dealers, and customers. Their feedback, not the *a priori* analysis of market data for the country, then forms the basis for expansion into the market. Thus, Honda decided to sell its small motorbikes only after American buyers asked for them. Canon moved into specialty camera stores after many personal visits over several months to alternative outlets. A senior executive with entrepreneurial spirit who knew very little about how cars were sold in America spearheaded Nissan's entry there. Shiseido lingered for many years on the drugstore counters before shifting to an upscale image.

UNCERTAINTY AND FLEXIBILITY

Why, after years of experience abroad, would the Japanese continue the intuitive incrementalist approach? The underlying explanation is partly that the Japanese feel insecure when relying on host country talent.[55] They don't think that they can ever really know and predict the people working for them—or that the local employees can really understand the Japanese.

This also helps explain why the Japanese employees who return from graduate study abroad rarely are sent back to the country they studied in. They may not even be sent abroad for some time. During the two years of study, they have been influenced and changed by fellow students and new ideas. They have experiences and perspectives that may be difficult for other Japanese to understand and accept. The returnees have to be "depressurized and debriefed" to fit into the organization again. If they are sent abroad right away, communication with headquarters in Japan will be difficult, since no one at home can really understand them and so cannot trust them.

A Western company entering a new country market generally looks for some qualified locals to set up distribution and marketing. When Kentucky Fried Chicken entered Japan, a key move was to hire a young but very capable Japanese to manage the operation. A Western manager either feels sufficiently at ease judging people from a foreign country, or believes that enforcing the appropriate contract stipulations can make a relationship reliable. Not so with the Japanese. Their way of business relies much more on personal relationships and an intimate understanding of the other person. Entering a foreign market is a painstaking and incremental process of discovering for yourself. They might collect a lot of information about a new market—but can still be very tentative about the entry. Where in the West impatience makes managers move decisively after a certain amount of time and resources have been spent, the Japanese will still commit only gradually.

If the Japanese lack foreign knowledge, then how do they succeed so often? The short answer is: by applying themselves diligently. The Japanese themselves think that this sets them apart from Westerners, especially the Europeans. Not having the confidence about foreign markets that the Europeans do, and without the hubris that sometimes afflicts Westerners, the Japanese, despite their successes, always feel uncertain about the new reality in a foreign country. For example, in the mid–1980s one of us was part of a comparative study of Swedish and Japanese subsidiaries in the United States.[56] The confidence about knowing the American market was palpable among the Swedes, much less so among the Japanese. In one Swedish firm there was "no time for market research," while in one Japanese company in a related industry the fax machine was constantly in use sending news and market information back to Japan. In answer to a direct question about Japanese competition, a spokesperson for Saab, the automaker, suggested that the Japanese automakers were not in the same league as Saab, and were not competitors. The head of Volvo's American subsidiary echoed the same sentiment in a TV interview at about the same time: "You have to be what you are. A company has to be true to itself, to what it represents." Within the year Honda had launched its Acura Legend, later followed by Toyota's Lexus and Nissan's Infiniti, luxury cars that dramatically changed the image of Japanese automakers and directly challenged the upscale European imports.

In the same study we also interviewed Japanese executives in the United States, at Sony in New Jersey, Toyota in California, and at less well-known companies such as Jamco and Atlas, smaller suppliers to the aircraft and transportation industries. Even in companies very successful in the U.S. market, managers always emphasized the need to update market knowledge. The Toyota spokesperson we interviewed was driving a competitor's car and talked glowingly about it. "We want to make as good a car ourselves," was the sentiment. Sony's Akio Morita always tried to catch the bus when in New York City, to be able to see how the end users of his company's products used them: the Sam Walton style again. The battle is ongoing; victory is never secure.

While the Swedes were very comfortable in the United States, the Japanese were generally uncomfortable—sometimes happily so, because one can argue, as some of them did, that comfort dulls the motivational edge. In interviews this thinking is often related to the experiences after World War II. Starting from scratch comes naturally to Japanese managers with memories of the devastation after the war. They turn weakness to advantage. You always hear that this will change when a new generation takes over. However, the socialization forces from family and school have so far overridden the tendency to individual assertiveness, and coupled with the insecurity engendered by the very real threat of natural disasters (earthquakes, typhoons), they have helped prevent immediate gratification from coming into fashion in Japan.

But a motivation to work hard and to pursue intuitive incrementalism is not always sufficient to beat informed *a priori* strategic thinking:

• You commit simple mistakes because the first step is so quick. For example, Honda's team arrived in the United States at the end of the motorcycle season.

• You don't always screen out obvious losing strategies because you don't take time to look at the whole end-to-end picture. Shiseido, the cosmetics maker, decided to enter the U.S. market through drugstores, not a bad strategy since the majority of the sales are made there. But the company tried to sell directly to American drugstore chains without first penetrating the key metropolitan markets. Only after hiring an American executive from rival Helena Rubinstein did the company realize that the buyers for drugstore chains bought what they saw in the upscale department stores in New York. The door to the drugstores in the Midwest was at Saks 5th Avenue.

• You don't properly anticipate problems, because you think you can always fix it later. When Mitsubishi Real Estate bought Rockefeller Center in the late 1980s, the executives thought they were doing the United States a favor. The company had been approached by the American owners and were happy to help out. There were intimations that the U.S. public would not be so happy about the sale, but the Japanese were excited by the opportunity to buy a landmark trophy. Furthermore, since this was in the heady days of the Japanese real estate boom, there would be plenty of buyers to sell to if they needed to exit. According to company spokesmen, the company was taken by surprise at the strength of the negative American reaction, and executives privately admitted they made a mistake. But pulling out became a headache, since the bubble had burst; there were no buyers, and in 1995 Mitsubishi walked away from it all.

But hard work, keeping your ear to the ground, quickly getting into action, and learning from your mistakes have two other great advantages. They make the managers less constrained by the "grand strategy," and help them adjust more quickly to changing conditions. They induce flexibility and speed.

Exhibit 4:1 helps explain this process. The Western approach to problem solving is systematic and deliberate: define the problem, develop

alternative solutions, evaluate each solution, choose strategy, and implement. For example, when selecting a foreign market to enter, the decision makers go through several cycles of meetings and the process
involves the collection of hard market data. In the evaluation stage several alternative markets and entry modes might be evaluated, comparing
the pros and cons of exporting directly, investing in an assembly plant, or
creating a joint venture. Systematic analysis is all to the good, but it
makes for a lot of boring meetings over the planning period. In the last
step the chosen strategy is implemented, with the allocation of appropriate resources, the creation of new positions, new managerial assignments, and so on. The process is logical, rational, even quasi-scientific.

Exhibit 4:1
The Key to Flexibility

Analytical Style			
Western Rationality	Defining and structuring the problem	Evaluating and finding one good solution	Implementing the solution
Japanese Incrementalism	Discuss the problems, devise solutions and implementation	Discuss the problems, devise solutions and implementation	Discuss the problems, devise solutions and implementation

6   12   . 18
Months

By contrast, the Japanese incrementalist approach involves very intensive group discussions (in so-called 1,000-cigarette meetings), followed
by the implementation of a small decision. Compared to those in the
West, the meetings are interminable, discussion is rambling, and there is
no clear agenda. But the meetings are scrounged together, and work with
a kind of exhaustion rationale. Suddenly, the leader will say that everybody has had a say; the next step is clear; roles are assigned or, more
often, assumed, and never clarified exactly, since everybody knows what
is expected and required. But while the meetings are long, in real time
the process may take less than a week, while the Western approach usu-

66 RELENTLESS

ally involves months, which means that participants scatter and have to be replaced, there is a need for updating, and for two steps forward there is always one step back.

The results from the action decided upon are discussed immediately by the Japanese, the evidence evaluated in more interminable meetings, and new—still small—decisions are taken. The cycle repeats itself as new feedback is obtained, and the company can change its course several times before the Western company has committed itself to one particular course of action.

This explains why an incremental entry approach squares with the swift Japanese approach to strategic adjustments. Where broad thinking about possibilities in an uncertain future takes place, the Japanese feel uneasy. But once the Japanese define the task and remove the uncertainties about what they should do, they execute with their customary adroitness.

When a lot of planning resources, time, and egos have been invested, a change in the strategy can be very traumatic both financially and personally. The incremental manager avoids this hassle. The Japanese consensus-style decision process serves to protect individuals from blame, and the lack of a planned strategy means that obstacles to adjustment are fewer. When feedback from the market mandates change, the Japanese organization responds immediately. No heads have to roll.

SPEED OF EXECUTION

But there is more to the Japanese successes. When market conditions change rapidly, competitors need to adjust their strategies quickly. Prices might have to be reduced, advertising campaign themes shifted, in-store promotions implemented, and new product introductions delayed or speeded up. Whether it is the entry of a new competitor, a new product, or some exogenous factor such as an unexpected oil crisis or the eruption of a war, if the demand or supply conditions change, the company might have to adjust or even abandon its planned strategy.

It is the immediate execution advantage that makes the incremental approach flexible. Speed and flexibility are at a premium when markets change. Whereas the grand-strategy view is appropriate for entry into a stable market, it is useless in markets where consumers change their preferences rapidly. This is where it leads to the paralysis-by-analysis problem, when the Western marketers waiting for the quarterly market research reports are reacting too slowly. "Close to the customer" means nothing unless changes can be implemented quickly.

Exhibit 4:2 illustrates this phenomenon. In the diagram, the changes in the market are depicted as a segment trajectory of changing preferences.

Where a strong Western analysis can help pinpoint exactly where the target is at the beginning, the Japanese hit-or-miss incrementalism will generally take some time before zeroing in on the target. However, as the preferences change over time, the Western company will soon be off-target, while the constant adjustments by the Japanese more nearly track the customer trajectory. The Western company will generally wait for its strategy to be off-target by some certain magnitude before reacting, and it will then make more of a quantum leap. But if the market keeps changing, this will still not be a good tracking strategy.

The book by Stalk and Hout about the importance of competing on time provides good evidence and useful tactics on how to speed up.[57] One problem with reacting quickly in Western markets tends to be that markets move more slowly than in Japan. According to personal interviews with managers at Toyota, Canon, and Matsushita, for example, some Japanese companies have had to slow down their market moves in the United States because it takes time to roll out products and promotional campaigns and to diffuse new information effectively in such a geographically large marketplace.

Exhibit 4:2
Incremental versus Strategic Adaptation

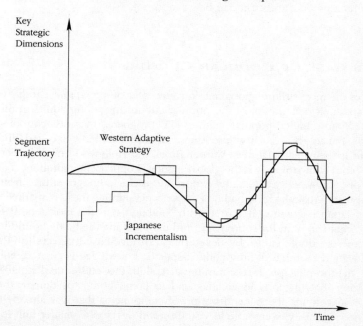

Western-style strategic planning makes most sense when the market is fairly stable over time, when there is no particular payoff to speed and flexibility. Likewise, one can see that one way for the Western company to improve its tracking is to shorten its reaction time, and reduce the magnitude of the changes. The current emphasis on speed and competing on time is therefore a natural response to Japanese competition. As European markets open up further, the Japanese will force long-dominant domestic companies to shed their fat and become lean and mean—just what the Europeans seem to dread.

Following shifting customer preferences is of course not the only game in town. In markets where technology leads preferences, the leading company naturally is in the forefront of technology. This does not involve only industrial high-tech, but also consumer technology such as telecommunications and consumer electronics. Then, rather than staying close to customers—the natural posture of the incrementalist who reacts quickly—the company might stay close to the technology.[58] The company then becomes a "pro-active" marketer, offering new products that have yet to demonstrate their acceptance in the marketplace. Such a company—Sony is one of a few like this in Japan, being an innovative technology leader—is not only an incremental marketer as described above, but in marketing terms is a technology-oriented company, welding together a product and customer orientation.

THE CASE OF POPULAR CULTURE

One of the most striking global market successes of the Japanese today is perhaps their penetration of the popular culture for young adults in the West. Young adults' popular culture—TV programs, mascots, cartoons, games, music—is an area where American marketers have excelled, and where it seems as if Disney, Warner Bros., the Hollywood moguls, and the record companies own the global market. Popular entertainment is in fact one of America's leading export industries. Foreign efforts from Europe and Australia have had little success penetrating the U.S. market.

But Japan is coming. It started with Nintendo's arcade monsters, battling American Atari for supremacy, and then shifting the battleground to in-home electronic games by developing cartridge-based players for TV use, a good example of how context-specific knowledge is created, and how me-too-plus product churning can shift the entire marketplace. Realizing that the kids in arcades had to come home for dinner, the Japanese, through the miniaturization of components that was already a Japanese specialty, were able to visualize and develop a smaller unit for home use. As Atari folded, Nintendo then developed the hand-held electronic game, the Gameboy, a huge success that again drew on intuition and existing know-how. The only surprising thing about the appearance of a strong Japanese competitor, Sega, is how long it took. Now, with two strong Japanese competitors going head to head—lean enterprises "colliding," in Robin Cooper's phrase—the churning has reached dizzying speeds.[59]

Consumer electronics being a Japanese core competence, the successes of Nintendo and Sega are perhaps understandable. More surprising is the success of Japanese cartoon figures and animated features on Western children's television, especially since the upbringing and schooling of Japan's children are hardly typical of what is done in the West.

Cartoons have a long tradition in Japan, and *manga*, the Japanese magazines filled with cartoons, have also become quite popular among some Western habitués. But the real story is in animation. The Japanese style, featuring a minimum of dialogue but a maximum of emotion and action, is easily recognized from the characters' large black eyes. Japanese *anime* (for animation) emphasizes facial expression much more than the typical Disney animated feature, and the characters' faces are outsized relative to the bodies. As a consequence, the cartoons become close-ups, making communication without words quite easy. A huge tear, a bleeding finger, a broken shoe do not need words, just as Charlie Chaplin discovered in silent films years ago. Furthermore, in a subtle twist, characters rarely are shown from the side, facing each other, the way Western dialogue is often conceived, whether it is Cinderella talking to her fairy godmother or to the stepmother sending her to the loft. Instead of making you an observer of a confrontation, in Japanese cartoons you either see the characters facing you or you see their backs, making audience empathy and involvement very natural—and apparently globally understood.

An artist like Hayao Miyazaki challenges even Disney with feature-length movies about the exciting but innocent adventures of small girls, braggart boys, and cute animals. According to box office figures, when going against a Disney animated feature in Japan, Miyazaki wins. His *My Neighbor Totoro*, about two young girls who are befriended by a furry creature who flies around in a bus shaped like a cat, has become a success in the United States after its introduction in 1994. The next arrival was *Sailor Moon*, in 1995, the story of a junior high school girl who, when needed, is transformed into long-legged super-heroine, and together with her "sailor" friends, all girls, conquers all evil. The theme of women's superiority is not uncommon in Japanese cartoons, and the fact that girls are winners helps to underline the popular "underdogs win" theme. But these girls are hardly feminists; they wear makeup, go-go boots, and miniskirts, all planned marketing that has set off a boom in crossover merchandising.

Sailor Moon is a leading program in France. So is *Mighty Morphin Power Rangers*, the program that has swept the global market and is popular in many countries, including the United States. The *Power Rangers* is a nonanimated show that features a team of schoolchildren who are transformed—the transformation theme again—into fighters for the right against various monsters and intruders from outer space. A distant relative of the old *Godzilla* movies, the program has become a favorite of Western kids, and in 1994 at Christmastime, for birthdays, and at Halloween, *Power Rangers* products were favorite items. Bandai, the Japanese company that produces the merchandise associated with the show, is not well-known outside Japan, but is Japan's largest toymaker. Between 1993 and 1995, the dolls and accessories sold by its American subsidiary were the most popular toys in the United States.

These successes do not come from careful product planning and painstaking analysis of market data. They emerge from many tries, some hits and many misses, just like the typical TV sitcoms in the United States. Popular appeal is difficult to predict, even for the Japanese. But what these successes have in common is a decided emphasis on audience involvement and liking. And they know that such emotions can come from the slightest shift of perspective, and a different angle. The globally successful Hello Kitty doll, from Sanrio, is often perceived to be their closest friend by the girls who buy it. How was such a strong positioning achieved? By giving the doll no mouth, so that the owner could read into Hello Kitty's face whatever emotion she herself felt at the moment. Intuitive marketing.

Who Needs a Strategy?

The lack of strategy in the Japanese approach has not cost them as much as Westerners might have anticipated. Their focus on implementation and execution has worked very well in many instances. To see why that is, it is useful to spell out when strategy is needed.

THE STRATEGY IMPERATIVE

The reasons that strategy has become important to Western companies are of course many and varied. The early works include Alfred P. Sloan Jr.'s account of his work at General Motors, and Alfred Chandler's linking of structure to strategy in four American companies. In essence, the typical large firm, a multidivisional and multinational entity operating in several industries and countries, needs to develop a systematic calculus to compare operations in different industries along common dimensions for coordination and control. Strategic management became a matter of setting objectives, budgeting resources, and comparing performance against forecasts. Later, the well-known Boston Consulting Group (BCG) growth-share matrix became a tool for handling complex tradeoffs between strategic business units.

Increased international competition in many markets, not the least from Japan, has further emphasized the need for smart revenue-increasing and cost-efficient strategies, for companies to stay competitive. The technology, both hardware and software, to formulate and implement strategies, even globally, has developed on a massive scale. Strategic business thinking has been credited with such impressive and varied feats as the global growth of McDonald's fast food, the sustained successes of large companies such as Hewlett-Packard, Daimler-Benz, and Benetton, and even the takeover of many world markets by Japanese firms.

The Japanese firms do of course have strategic visions and objectives, even though their actual plans of operation—especially in marketing—tend to be less detailed, not written down, and in general based on intuition more than on hard analysis of quantitative data. As we have seen, they are incremental, they imitate competition, and they place themselves below the customers. Is this really their recipe for success?

STRATEGY, IMPLEMENTATION, AND EXECUTION

To understand why the Japanese have succeeded as intuitive incrementalists, it is important to answer the question: When is strategy necessary? Generically, strategy means a certain amount of premeditation before action, an evaluation of (and choice between) alternative paths to a goal, and a spelling out of the steps to reach the destination. These features characterize most strategic situations facing a firm, Japanese as well as Western, in manufacturing, marketing, or any other function. The distinction between strategy *formulation* and strategy *implementation* is also important. Roughly speaking, the issue is between what to do and how to do it. Most textbooks talk about strategy formulation—deciding which alternative to choose—and relatively few speak to the issue of implementation. Why? Implementation requires an understanding of the context in which the strategy is to be executed, and thus does not lend itself easily to a treatment in terms of principles.[60]

The Japanese as a rule do not pay too much attention to strategy *formulation* in marketing. But they pay a lot of attention to *implementation* in marketing. That is, they focus much more on how to do it than on what should be done. Major decisions, such as Nissan's entry into the U.S. market, or the acquisitions of foreign firms, such as the purchase by Matsushita of MCA Communications, might have been done without in-depth analysis of alternative uses of the funds, but there is no doubt that a lot of resources went into implementing them successfully (including high salaries for American top managers).

In fact, the Japanese add another category to the strategic breakdown. This is *execution*. If the strategy formulation is what to do and implementation is how to do it, execution is doing it. In other words, the strategy could be to defend a market position by speeding up the introduction of new product variants. The implementation might consist of the creation of task force teams to focus on various new technologies and the establishment of cross-functional management committees to facilitate information exchanges among R&D, manufacturing, and marketing. Execution then involves the actual development and launch of new products at a rapid pace. A similar distinction is of course used in team sports. The strategy in World Cup soccer might be to play defense, and rely on counterattacks to score. To implement the strategy a midfielder might be given a defensive assignment, and long balls will be used to reach two lone strikers up front. The execution is then a question of how these key players perform on the field. Exhibit 4:3 suggests some dimensions of marketing decision making and how they fall into the three categories.

Exhibit 4:3
Execution as "Doing" Marketing

Thinking

Strategy Formulation   High-end niche; uniform across countries;
"What to do"   global presence.

Strategy Implementation   Limited product line; products standardized;
"How to do it"   superior service; training for sales/repair staff;
                                 high base salary for salespeople; global brand name;
                                 prototype advertising.

Doing

Execution   What brand name? What advertising message?
"Do it"   Actual base salary; select what models to feature;
                                 meet the customer; make a sale.

Thus, the stage of actually executing a strategy is separable from the two preceding stages, and in many cases the most important one. In particular, execution becomes important when analyzing the Japanese marketers because of their emphasis on incrementalism, and learning by doing.

STRATEGY BY POLICY

If you have no choice, you don't need to formulate a strategy. If only one path to the destination is feasible or otherwise acceptable, you simply have to specify the goal, spell out how to get there, and then do it. This may not be easy either—but it has to do with implementation and execution, not strategy formulation.

Some examples will help show that this is not an unlikely case. When Nissan decided to enter the United States, it may well be that the company had no choice. If Nissan had made an overriding policy decision to follow the leading company, Toyota, the issues facing Nissan were more those of implementation and execution. Matsushita faced the same predicament in deciding to buy MCA, since Sony had already bought Columbia Pictures. Thus, the competitive parallelism characterizing many Japanese companies has the effect of eliminating the need for strategy formulation.

If one considers the situation in Japan after World War II and after the Korean War, it is clear that very few strategic choices were feasible. Those strategies that were chosen involved government support, cooperation between companies in the same industry, and so on, in patterns well-described elsewhere.[61] The catching up with the West involved choices that were rarely made by the individual companies (although the companies did not always heed the government directions—as in the case of the auto companies, for example). Nevertheless, in either case the cornerstone of the strategy was to learn from the successful Western companies and license their technology. There was little need for in-depth strategy formulation, although the stories from the actors about the implementation and execution of the strategy makes for entertaining and interesting reading. For a particularly striking example of the early kamikaze approach, the development of a video recorder for home use by Sony is instructive.

In the early 1950s, American companies had already lost considerable amounts of money on video for home use. CBS reportedly lost $30 million on its Electronic Video Recording (EVR), an $800 device that permitted viewers to play cartridges on their television sets. Ampex, the leader in the industry, selling mainly to broadcasting stations, had tried and was not able to launch a home video unit. Later, Cartridge Television's Cartrivision, one of the largest financial debacles of the 1960s, played movies and, by a skip-field method, could record television programs. It lost $60 million.

In the early 1960s, Sony licensed the Ginsburg patent, the key invention that converted video signals to FM signals, then recorded them on tape, from Ampex. Within months, a project development team in Tokyo had developed the first version of what was to become the Betamax machine. Gradually improving picture quality and ease of use, and with lower price and compact size, Sony introduced the definitive version of Betamax in May 1975. At $600, it became an instant best-seller—although the first units were bought by Japan Victor Company, a subsidiary of Matsushita, the Osaka-based giant electronics firm, which proceeded to reverse-engineer the machine and developed the finally dominant VHS system, another example of no-holds-barred kamikaze competition.[62]

In recent years there has of course been a much greater need for the Japanese firms to develop independent strategies. This is where one is particularly struck by their willingness to do strategy by policy. Thus, when Honda decided to assemble cars in the U.S. market because the home market was too crowded—a truly strategic decision—the reason that carried the day was Soichiro Honda's own conviction. When Sony decided to market the Walkman, Akio Morita went against the research and ordered the launch. Toshiba introduced the laptop computer against its own field reports that no U.S. customer wants a PC with such inferior picture resolution.[63]

Thus clear-cut needs, overriding company policy, and imitation of the competition make strategy formulation less important for the Japanese firms. Similarly, the concentration in one industry rather than several makes it less necessary to create formalized planning systems—only conglomerate companies such as Toshiba are said to use some kind of strategic business unit (SBU) portfolio organizational structure.

Today Japanese companies need to make many strategic marketing choices. For example, the integration of Europe poses many dilemmas for the Japanese, who would like to participate in some way in the expected market expansion. Should they invest in assembly or continue exporting? In which country should the European headquarters be located? What about Eastern European developments versus placing an assembly plant in Portugal? And so on. Of course, we know already that the Japanese firms tend to follow one another, but there is still a fair amount of discretionary choice. Don't they need strategy for these decisions?

COMMITMENT AND REVERSIBILITY

The need for strategic premeditation in the face of a choice situation is proportionate to the level of commitment involved and the degree to which the action is reversible.[64] Commitment has two aspects: magnitude of commitment and length of time of commitment. The larger the commitment and the longer the time period involved, the greater the need for strategic planning. As for reversibility, if the decision is easily reversed, there is little need for strategic analysis. Reversibility requires both ability and willingness to reverse a course of action.

The relationship between commitment and reversibility is shown in Exhibit 4:4. Mainly in the case of large commitments and irreversibility is there a strong need for strategic analysis. For the Japanese incrementalists who are satisfied to take one step at a time and who are flexible enough to change course in midstream, the need for strategy is lessened. Compare that to the Western managers who measure their self-worth by the stakes involved in their decision making, and who believe that a chosen strategy must play itself out before any changes are contemplated. The Japanese do not need strategy to the same extent as the Western companies.

Exhibit 4:4

The Need for Strategy: The Role of Commitment

$$\text{Need for Strategy} = \left[\frac{\text{Level of}}{\text{Commitment}} - \frac{\text{Reversibility}}{\text{of Action}} + \frac{\text{Predictability}}{\text{of Outcome}} \right]$$

$$\text{Level of Commitment} = \left[\begin{array}{l} \text{Magnitude of Commitment (\$)} \\ \text{Length of Commitment (time)} \end{array} \right.$$

$$\text{Reversibility of Actions} = \left[\begin{array}{l} \text{Willingness to Change} \\ \text{Ability to Change} \end{array} \right.$$

$$\text{Predictability of Outcome} = \text{Predictability of} \left[\begin{array}{l} \text{Speed and} \\ \text{Magnitude} \end{array} \right] \text{of Change}$$

PREDICTABILITY

But many strategic choices for the Japanese do involve large commitments and are irreversible. In fact, many accounts of their involvement overseas stress their willingness to commit for the long haul, and the amount of resources made available. When Marubeni, the large trading company, helps Iran build a refinery, it is to the tune of an initial outlay of $300 million, and its Japanese expatriates are the last outsiders to leave the country as Khomeini takes power. When Sony according to most analysts overpays for acquisition of Columbia Pictures, Norio Ohga claims that in the long run the purchase will benefit everybody in the company, something that still has to be shown. Panasonic's takeover of the old Motorola TV plant outside Chicago still ranks as one of Matsushita's most expensive endeavors ever, but Matsushita continues to honor the initial commitment to the workforce twenty years later. And so on.

The reason there seems to have been so little strategy in these decisions is simply lack of predictability. For premeditation of alternative strategies to be useful, there has to be a way of predicting what might happen given alternative choices. With little or no way of knowing what will happen, there is little reason to try to be analytical and smart (unless one is willing to see strategy as a game under uncertainty, decide on a mixed strategy solution, and then roll the dice to come up with a strategy).

Given their background as experienced "amateurs" in marketing and their lack of belief in formal marketing research, the Japanese suspect all Western-style predictions and forecasts. Most marketing predictions usually factor in three separable components: (1) exogenous events, such as the state of the economy and consumer expectations, (2) competitors' actions, and (3) the firm's own actions. Thus, in many if not most marketing choice situations, a company must forecast not only exogenous events but also competitive actions and the market's response to the firm's own marketing mix (see Exhibit 4:5).

Exhibit 4:5

Predictability

$$\left[\text{Speed and Magnitude of Changes} \right] = f \left[\text{Own actions, Competitors' actions, Exogenous shifts} \right]$$

(Exogenous shifts include economic and political changes, shifts in taxes, key success factors, etc.)

Predictability requires

1. knowledge about market response:
   • to own actions
   • to competitors' actions
   • to exogenous shifts

2. predictions (forecasts) of
   • competitors' actions
   • exogenous shifts

and 3. stability of the market response over time.

Lack of knowledge about and experience in many foreign markets means low predictability, and helps explain why there was a lack of strategic analysis in several of these cases. For the Japanese, outcomes must have been extremely difficult to assess *a priori*, and only adherence to some overriding objective or vision could justify the choices made. Furthermore, given the intense competition among the Japanese, and the lack of experience with non-Japanese competitors, one can see why prediction of outcomes would be difficult (although perhaps not prediction of competitive reaction—hindsight shows that domestic competitors are unlikely to respond, and Japanese competitors are almost certain to follow).

While the competitive reaction possibilities do not explain why the Japanese are nonstrategic at home, a related problem for predictability affects both foreign and home markets. This is stability of responses over time. For analytical predictions to be made, one needs a certain level of stability in the various response functions over time. Thus, one would require consumer responses to marketing mix decisions, and competitive reactions to our firm's moves, to exhibit the same pattern tomorrow as yesterday and today—or, at the minimum, any changes would in themselves be predictable.

Unpredictability and instability of market response are of course factors that affect Western companies as well. Mistakes in market judgment and timing by IBM, Apple, GM, and other companies tend to generate a feeding frenzy among newspaper reporters. The Japanese are not spared. When Honda introduced the Acura Legend in March 1986, initial sales were slower than expected. The *Wall Street Journal* wondered if Honda had not "stumbled." The idea of a Japanese luxury car was "a marketing flop," said Volvo North America's CEO in an interview.[65] "The Japanese cannot compete against the European luxury cars" was the common refrain. The Acura name was pronounced unpronounceable.

As history has shown, such judgments were premature. True to incrementalism, Honda regrouped, increased dealer coverage and advertising expenditures, trained dealers in giving outstanding service, won the customer satisfaction battle against Mercedes, and used the J. D. Power CSI (customer satisfaction index) as a key competitive weapon to make Legend a success. As Mark Twain said: "The reports of my death are greatly exaggerated."

Exhibit 4:6 summarizes the arguments supporting the lack of strategic inclination among the Japanese companies. With turbulence in the markets (also in Japan) because of international competition and deregulation, with rapid changes in technology, the speeding up of product life cycles, and so on, it is little wonder that the Japanese don't believe that responses are stable. In fact, the success of their intuitive incrementalism depends on this very issue, as we have seen. Intuition based on experience may not have been an acceptable alternative for Western managers in the past. They needed to be professionals, with skills to manage the most diverse set of businesses. But in today's competitive marketplace there is no substitute for managers who have experience with the products, intuition about customers, and judgment about competitors. Ask Apple. Ask Sears. Ask Chrysler, GM, and Ford. Ask Microsoft. Ask Novell about WordPerfect. Ask IBM and Lotus. Ask AT&T. Ask the "amateur" Japanese managers at home and in overseas markets. Good businesspeople can understand their customers intuitively.

Exhibit 4:6
The "Execution" No Strategy

Commitment:		A little at a time (incrementalism)
Reversibility:		Low exposure enables change
Predictability:	Learn	•by trial and error •about market (response) •about competitors •about customers
Product Strategy:	Imitate	•to avoid uncertainty •to match competitors
Competitive Strategy:	Churning	•to ruin the strategists •to run the market •to create new rules

5
TARGETING
COMPETITORS

One of the main themes throughout the first four chapters of this book has been the customer orientation of the Japanese marketers. The customer focus does not exclude a product orientation, and we have tried to show how staying close to the customer and using intuition have made it natural to infer customers' preferences by their behavior and reactions to new and existing products. So it may come as a surprise to learn that the Japanese companies are fundamentally competitor-driven. Kenichi Ohmae, the former McKinsey Japan executive, even chastises the Japanese for being too obsessed with competitors to pay proper attention to customers.[66]

There are two reasons for the competitor focus, both related to the peculiar conditions at home in Japan. One reason is the similarity of the firms' resource endowments. As we mentioned before, the lack of natural resources and the redistribution of assets after World War II have made people the main distinguishing resource for companies. This levels the playing field when they compete against one another and makes competition in Japan similar to a match between opposing sports teams, all playing according to the same rules (this does not hold true, of course, when they play against foreign competitors). The chase for market share among competitors in the home market in Japan is akin to an annual tournament, with the winners widely published in the media and resulting in enhanced employee pride, making it possible to attract better college graduates, who can marry better, and so on.

The second reason that companies are competitor-driven is that some-times they can afford to take their eyes off the customers at home. At least they could before the current recession and the emergence of the "new consumer," the one who buys made-in-America products, and doesn't worry about the lack of prestige in buying cheaper products. But even the new consumer seems to have one thing in common with the traditional customer: predictable similarity. Even if the young, new, and unconven-tional consumers are different, they are different in the same way. This includes not only the *Harajuku shinjin*, the young aspiring punk elements who appear in Tokyo on weekends, but also the new parents who drive Jeeps and buy fishing rods and boots from L. L. Bean, and the young peo-ple who all want Levi's and football jerseys, eat Häagen-Dazs ice cream and Kellogg's cereal, listen to Madonna, and watch Disney.

To be fair, the new conditions have made the market a little less pre-dictable than before. For example, Matsushita's market forecasts for new products in the Japanese market used to be very accurate, built up from dealer estimates and past experience. In a couple of recent cases, how-ever, their forecasts have turned out very wrong. For one product a fore-cast of 15,000 first-year units turned into actual sales of approximately 2,500. In another, a forecast of 2,000 to 3,000 units translated into orders for close to 50,000 units, a volume the company could not supply.[67] Toyota's simpler and less luxurious truck, initially a best-seller, started losing sales as soon as there were signs of an improving economy.

But overall, the homogeneity and predictability of the Japanese market is striking. When the recession hit in the early 1990s, everybody cut down on spending and started to save, exacerbating the downturn. The roots of such behavior are deep. Strong and consistent cultural and social influ-ences have made for little diversity of opinion and tastes. An even income distribution has induced the vast majority to consider themselves middle class. Lifestyle is a matter of age, sex, and stage in the life cycle. There is little differentiation in consumption behaviors. When new trends appear, they are embraced by all in the same age cohort. To the extent the young generation is "different," its members tend to be different in the same way.

This is why the Japanese companies tend to feel confident about what moves the Japanese consumers: the actions of their competitors. And once the market moves, the whole market will move. Keeping your eye on the ball means keeping your eye on competition.

COMPETITIVE CHURNING

Of course, both customers and competitors merit attention in any market-ing effort. But where consumer behavior is homogeneous, and competition is among firms with similar resource endowments, the companies naturally are driven more by predicted competitive action than by consumers. For example, when the 1985 New York Plaza accord among the seven major industrial nations lowered the dollar rate by 40 percent against the yen, the anticipated (and hoped for) price increases on Japanese goods in the United States did not materialize. The Japanese companies could simply not trust their Japanese competitors to raise prices as well. At Canon, the belief was that if it raised prices, Minolta would not, but would take share from them in the United States. The auto companies and the consumer electronics firms were caught in the same bind.

COMPETITIVE PARALLELISM

The parallelism between Japanese competitors' strategies can be seen by even a cursory observer of their actions in foreign markets, and it also has its counterpart at home in Japan. The imitation is not only of Japanese companies' actions but also of Western companies' strategies. The incrementalist attitudes go well with the close tracking of competitive moves, and the rapid imitation of marketing efforts, and leads to a "churning" effect in the marketplace.[68] The churning phenomenon involves quick imitations of new product entries by competitors, some competitors adding new features, the pioneering firm responding by upgrading the first entry, and competitors renewing the attack. The effect is a type of vicious high-speed tit-for-tat circle of new and modified product entries, intense proliferation of models, and continually lowered prices.

Examples of Japanese churning are almost unlimited. When Toyota entered the California market with its Corona in the early 1960s, it was modeled on the VW Beetle. The later introduction of Datsun's 200SX was modeled on the Corona. Among automakers these patterns still continue. The success of the Honda Accord in the late 1970s led to the Toyota Camry, the Nissan Stanza, and the Mazda 626. In cameras, Canon's automatic AE–1 of the mid-1970s was soon copied by the other makers, as was Minolta's Maxxum auto-focus camera ten years later. The Sony videocamera was soon followed by products from Matsushita, Sharp, and other firms. The Walkman was soon copied by all Japanese manufacturers, as was the Fuji introduction of transparent cassette housing for audiotape.

The churning phenomenon is similar to the "tornado" effect for Silicon Valley–style competition, described by Moore in *Inside the Tornado*.[69] The tornado is the competitive process through which the dominant standard in the marketplace is established. In Moore's Silicon Valley, this process involves an all-out marketing effort by competitors, each aiming to establish the standard, and only one being the winner. He points to IBM PC/DOS and how it was established as the dominant operating system as a typical example. A Japanese example is the format battle in videotape between Sony's Betamax and Matsushita's VHS. This war was won by VHS partly because of the longer recording time of its tapes, something that, incidentally, was a result of pressure from RCA, the U.S. licensee of the VHS technology, to record football games. The key move was the decision by Matsushita not only to license the VHS system to competitors, as Sony had done with its Betamax system, but also to provide the key components for the licensees. Sony learned the lesson, and when the 8mm videocam was introduced, it followed the same strategy, creating a much more sustainable advantage that is holding Matsushita at bay.

The bitter battle between these two companies, Sony from Tokyo and Matsushita from Osaka, reflects traditional feuding between Edo (Tokyo) and Kansai (Osaka), which spills over into marketing. A current example is the advertising for videocameras. As a natural strategy, Matsushita is trying to leverage off its vast VHS base of VCRs when selling its branded JVC, Panasonic, and National videocameras. Matsushita's advertising in the United States and elsewhere long claimed that its videocameras are the only ones that can record tapes for playback on a VHS machine, confusing buyers by ignoring the fact that the 8mm tapes from Sony and its licensees (Canon, Sanyo, and others) are easily transferable to a VHS recorder.

According to Moore, there is only one winner in the tornado, as the other companies will have to change to the new standard. However, as we will show below, the identity of the winner in the churning war in Japan is usually not so clear, because the differences in the technology employed are usually not so sharp. The patent protection in Japan works differently than in the United States. While in the United States the aim is to protect the inventor's right to control the use of the invention, in Japan the patent process is aimed at diffusing technology as quickly and as widely as possible among Japanese companies. This is one reason the VHS system could compete so quickly with the Sony invention. The first buyers of Sony's Betamax were engineers at Japan Victor Company (JVC), a subsidiary of Matsushita. The fact that the Betamax and VHS are incompatible owes more to the stubbornness and conflicting personalities of the two company leaders, Akio Morita at Sony and Konosuke Matsushita, than it does to technological uniqueness. The churning practiced by the Japanese usually endorses the newest technology and goes one step further to improve it. And then another step. And another. This is why churning does not have only one winner—and also why the game never ends. In fact, you could almost say that the Japanese create the same competitive conditions in mature markets as are the rule in fast-moving high-tech markets, with new innovations constantly introduced to the market.

FIRST-MOVER DISADVANTAGE?

Because of churning, being first in the Japanese marketplace may not yield the typical first-mover advantage. Companies such as Matsushita and Toyota have done very well without many original or innovative products. Of course, there is evidence that the assumed loyalty to the first entrant, and the other advantages associated with first-movers, such as distribution tie-ups and more rapid accumulation of experience, are also overrated in Western markets.[70] But the speed and efficiency with which Japanese imitators enter a market are unprecedented. P&G's successful Pert shampoo with the new two-in-one formula (shampoo and conditioner, avoiding the need for separate treatments), introduced in the 1980s, had no follower in the American market for four years. Once it was introduced in the Japanese market, there were two competing brands within six months (from Kao and Unilever Japan, even though the latter's Western parent had not responded earlier in the U.S. market). In another six months, new brands on the market had three-in-one formulations (adding rinse), and the proliferation of me-too-plus-one products is continuing.[71]

Exhibit 5:1 depicts graphically how the first entrant is caught rapidly by imitative competitors, whose new features may wipe out any early advantage. It is a common pattern for Western innovators in Japan, such as P&G's Pampers, Braun's coffeemakers, and Unilever's Timotei shampoo, which all quickly lost large initial market shares to Japanese firms Uni-Charm, National (Matsushita), and Kao, respectively.

Rapid imitation requires close monitoring of market developments, something that the Japanese are good at, as we have already seen. It also requires rapid mobilization of company personnel and know-how to reverse-engineer the first-mover's new product and develop a clone. The flexibility of the Japanese incrementalism helps here, as does the fact that the technical know-how is usually already diffused. While Matsushita researchers had worked for over ten years to develop a videotape recorder, as had Sony's team, once the Betamax was on the market, JVC had a version working in less than six months, although the longer-recording VHS format took more time.

How can a company in Japan continue to innovate under this pressure? Good question. Sony's solution, according to Kozo Ohsone, who was lead developer of the Discman, the portable compact disc player, is simply to run faster, and keep adding features. With the exception of the Betamax, Sony's new products used to have up to eighteen months of lead time before competition entered. The Trinitron television had in fact a longer time, since the technology was not released to other companies, against standard Japanese practice. But today, according to Ohsone-san, Sony expects only around six months of a lead. Because of this, Sony has simply adopted the philosophy that it must churn against its own products, not worrying about cannibalizing existing winners with newer variants. The first-mover advantages can only be sustained by proliferation of new products. Hamel and Prahalad's concept of the "core competence" as the sustainable advantage, not the company's products as such, fits very well with this notion.[72] Sony's edge lies in its ability to innovate, not in the products themselves.

Exhibit 5:1
First-Mover Disadvantage

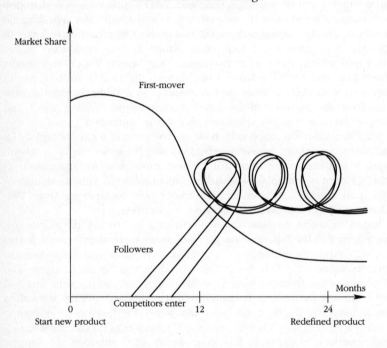

THE SYNERGY FROM RIVALRY

The immediate impact of the intense rivalry would seem to be negative for the firms. Porter, for example, uses a Japanese firm, Fujitsu, as an example of a "bad" competitor.[73] Similarly, the focus on competition has prompted at least one Japanese commentator to complain about whether some Japanese companies really understand that a customer orientation is a more appropriate philosophy for a business.[74] The Japanese companies ruin profit margins, oversupply niches in the market, generate over-capacity in the industry, and do not attempt to serve properly an as-yet unfilled need. Western competitors, by contrast, take an economically more viable perspective, focusing on innovation and uniqueness and having something of a live-and-let-live approach.

There is no doubt about the validity of some of Porter's points. The Japanese themselves acknowledge their ruinous corporate behaviors in industries such as steel and shipbuilding, where new investments continued long after the markets were saturated, and even in some consumer electronics markets (the desperate wars in audio and video recorders and tape are good examples). Few of the several Japanese firms selling magnetic tape—TDK, Maxell, Fuji, Sony, and others—make money on that business. Seiko, the large watchmaker, competing against Citizen, Casio, and the rejuvenated Swiss and American watchmakers, has lost money on watches most years in the last decade (making up the losses with its success with Epson printers). When the market is glutted and prices come down to rock bottom, companies might not survive (even though the low prices are good for the consumer—at least in the short run).

But there are competitive benefits to the intense Japanese rivalry, benefits that accrue to the Japanese companies as a group and become a Japanese advantage against the West. Paradoxically enough, these "synergistic" benefits have been ignored by commentators, perhaps because they are so obvious.[75] Everybody knows that the Japanese have been very successful—but how have they done it if their rivalry has been so "bad" for profitability? The theoretical explanation is that they first have eliminated Western competition (which is largely correct), and that they then have raised prices to recoup their losses (which they have not done). So, how did they do it?

The explanation hinges on synergistic effects on both the demand and supply sides. Exhibit 5:2 summarizes the main points.

Exhibit 5:2
Results from Churning

Demand Side
1. Defines (or redefines) what features the core product or service should have.
2. Changes preferences for styling, design, etc. (because of "pure exposure" effect).
3. Educates customers generically about the products and how to evaluate them.
4. Offers customers the benefit of genuine competition.

Supply Side
1. Diffuses new technology rapidly through many opportunities for application.
2. Educates the suppliers in the new technology.
3. Enables large-scale training for service and after-sales repairs.
4. Justifies investments in new component manufacturing (high utilization).

First, the demand side. As several Japanese introduce similar new products in a market there will be a "pure exposure" effect on consumers. That is, even if the new designs are radical—and many are not, given the incremental approach—consumers will get used to seeing the new designs. As in the fashion world, this allows the consumers to become accustomed to the new palette.

In the same way, Japanese companies, through the cumulative impact from their imitative strategy, point the consumers toward their new designs. One example is in automobile design. The wedge-shape car style, with a downward sloping front and high back, emerged with the front-wheel drive of the Volkswagen Golf/Rabbit and was reinforced by Honda's Accord and Prelude, soon followed by Toyota, Nissan, and Mazda. The radical new line soon became mainstream, with the "classic" style of a Chrysler K-car quaintly old-fashioned. But the front-wheel drive and the downward-sloping hood had already been in view for years—in the Swedish Saab. But the Saab was always a curiosity, loved by a small niche segment of the market, praised for its uniqueness. Contrast this with the churning by the Japanese. Without the Japanese, the Rabbit would in all likelihood have become the "new Beetle" it was intended to be, with a special segment of the market all to itself—and the mainstream styling would still come from Detroit. From this viewpoint, one would hope for Ford's sake that the new Taurus design inspires imitative competitors. Without copies, the new design may be too radical—with imitators, it will become "the original."

Western companies traditionally take a disdainful stance against imitation—the we-have-to-be-special attitude, which leads to the not-invented-here syndrome. "That's good for them, but it is not what we want to do—we are different," is the sentiment. Although the popularity of Japanese-style benchmarking (see below) suggests that this sentiment is weakening, Western marketers still preach the gospel of unique differentiation.

NEW DOMINANT DESIGN

Churning offers additional demand-side benefits. As the new products are introduced, not only customers need to be educated about the new features, but also salespeople and other middlemen. The similarity among the Japanese products leverages the training and education, with media exposure serving more than one manufacturer. Thus, the retailers and wholesalers learn what the new products are about, and can handle more than one company's products. Furthermore, as consumers learn what to look for, they automatically eliminate products without the newly salient features from their consideration. Toyota took some time accepting the shift to front-wheel drive, but finally introduced the Camry in an effort to join the market shift (as some American makes and Volvo have now also done, but not yet BMW and Mercedes). Uniquely designed brands are bypassed because of what they don't offer. In an interesting exception to the churning behavior, Sharp's daring introduction of the videocamera with a small TV screen has not yet been copied by other Japanese, making its acceptance slower than otherwise.

As the market settles on a new dominant design, chances are it will be the Japanese one. After all, several companies will offer that alternative, so that the customer can feel secure about after-sales service. Cognitive dissonance, the uncertainty of possibly having made the wrong choice, is low because there are many users with similar designs. The so-called exposure principle is at work here as well. As people see these products used, they start thinking that this is normal behavior. In the beginning the users look funny, but then norms change. The typing into an electronic notebook during a meeting, talking on a cellular phone on the street, jogging on main streets in a Spandex outfit with a Walkman, and sending e-mail instead of knocking on your neighbor's door are examples of activities that looked ridiculous some time back (still do, to us laggards).

Regardless, product similarities also make prices competitive, and the consumer finds better value in Japanese offerings—the traditional economic justification for intense competition. The occasional complaint is that everybody has the same kind of product—but the cost of uniqueness has gone up.

The similarity with Moore's "tornado" development of standards in high-tech is striking. The company that gets an advantage because major customers are settling on its design as standard should just "Ship! Don't segment. Don't customize." [76] But since the Japanese companies cannot easily keep technology away from other firms, and new features are easy to imitate, the winners are many, not simply a single company. So, while in PC software Microsoft Word becomes the dominant word-processing program, WordPerfect and WordStar are finished, but in cameras, all new fixed-lens cameras from Japan are automatic, have self-focusing zoom lenses, and are self-winding. The recent attempt to establish a new type of camera to replace the 35mm is an example of the Japanese way, all companies following each other.

Churning also offers clear advantages on the supply side. The company can short-circuit several complex assembly tasks simply by checking what other companies have done by reverse engineering and benchmarking. Japan's different patent-granting and enforcement philosophy (which allows the diffusion of technology even though the patent application is still being processed, a time-consuming process), make the new technology as well as components and parts easily available, since the subcontractors can invest in new machine tools and equipment. Because all the companies introduce the new product, there is less reason for the suppliers to hold back on investments. To help justify such investments, members of *keiretsus*, the large groupings of firms prominent in the Japanese economy, are often allowed to sell to companies outside the group.

Saab, the Swedish automobile maker, again provides an illustrative example. Because of its unusual technology it was a high-risk purchase with uncertain and expensive service. After Honda and its Japanese followers made front-wheel drive standard, Saab technology and styling was no longer so different. Although this could have been to Saab's advantage, the company has not been able to capitalize on its first-mover status. The company, apparently focused on its small niche of loyal customers, has not adapted its strategy to face the fact that the erosion of its technological uniqueness makes it more mainstream.[77]

As a further result of the joint behavior, the components and parts will be available in quantity quickly, they will be tested out earlier, and the new products get on the market with fewer defects than usual. Japanese companies can introduce new products that function reliably from the first model year on. Many Western consumers traditionally wait for the first year's new car model or new camera or new TV set to "shake down," waiting to buy until the company has ironed out the bugs.

FOLLOW THE LEADER

Because of the tight monitoring of competitive moves among the Japanese, a tacit product leadership system develops.

PRODUCT LEADERSHIP

Although the leaders change over the years, most companies recognize the current leader as not necessarily the largest market share holder, but as the most innovative company. As in most homogeneous societies, comparisons are natural and relatively easy to make. In addition, Japanese newspapers periodically publish company rankings of various kinds—largest market share, number of employees, most desirable jobs, and so on. In consumer electronics, most Japanese companies monitor Sony's and now also Sharp's new products very closely. JVC and Matsushita could have taken the leadership with the VHS defeat of the Betamax, but Sony's rapid introduction of the Walkman and the championing of the winning CD format put Sony back on top. In autos, Toyota was viewed early as the new product leader because of its success in the U.S. market, but Honda took over when its Accord conquered the U.S. market at the end of the 1970s. Through the 1980s, Honda led with its innovative styling and its early foray into luxury cars with the Acura Legend, although the even greater success of the Lexus has Toyota challenging for the leadership. In cameras, Canon's leadership vanished when Minolta introduced the Maxxum, but recently the leadership has reverted to Canon as its "one-shot" models appeared. In yet another industry, Yamaha's unsuccessful challenge to Honda in motorcycles is well-documented.[78]

A striking example of a challenge to a market share leader and the ensuing reaction was the introduction of Asahi's "dry" beer in 1987.[79] Faced with declining share as number three in the domestic market after Kirin and Sapporo, and under attack from the newcomer Suntory, Osaka-based Asahi up through the early 1980s exhibited the typical traits of a loser, with lackluster products, weak new introductions, and sagging employee morale. The company's bank, Sumitomo, highly regarded after rescuing the Mazda corporation, decided in 1982 to take over the management of Asahi.

Upon his arrival from Sumitomo, Hirotaro Higuchi, a banker who had no previous experience in the beer industry, decided to invest in developing new and exciting beers, to rejuvenate the brand name among consumers, and to offer the existing distributors a more profitable opportunity. The first introduction, Asahi Draft, showed reasonable promise, but the Super Dry product, introduced in 1987, turned the company around. Drawing on existing research that showed that consumers in blind tests prefer beer with higher alcohol content, Asahi developed a new type of draft beer with the maximum allowable alcohol content (5.4 percent). Lower in sugar and less bitter than the traditional Japanese beer, including Kirin Lager, the market leader, and with sharper taste and lighter color, the new beer was positioned as the drink for more modern and younger consumers. The packaging, a metallic silver can with black lettering, and the name "Super Dry," hinting at the different taste, reinforced its image and positioning.

Going against traditional assumptions that the Japanese beer drinker wants heavy lagers to match the typically salty Japanese snacks and food, Asahi became an overnight sensation. Asahi's sales increased by 33 percent in 1987 as orders outran capacity; only about 70 percent of demand could be filled. Even though several of Asahi's existing breweries were quickly mobilized to produce Super Dry, potential sales were lost to competitors.

The competitors, who initially doubted the potency of the Super Dry threat, quickly regrouped. By the beginning of 1988, Kirin, Sapporo, and

Suntory all introduced me-too dry beers. New product introductions and advertising expenditures increased as competition heated up. After years of inactivity in major new introductions, Kirin and Sapporo intensified their new product development programs, and especially Kirin tested a number of new products in the Tokyo market. Failing to overcome Asahi's first-mover advantage with the original dry beer, Super Dry, Kirin finally hit with Ichiban Shibori (First Draft), a beer positioned between the heavy lagers and the new dry beers. Ichiban Shibori was introduced in 1991, two years after Asahi Super Dry, and with its sales added to the established lager brand, Kirin regained market leadership in the Japanese beer industry.

Fundamentally, such a "beer war" is a struggle for market share leadership, not necessarily for product leadership. But because of the product focus of the competitive strategies, the winner will de facto set the dominant product design standard. The synergy from intense rivalry comes exactly because of the product leadership-followership patterns.

THE COST OF UNIQUENESS

As we have seen, the insistent followership among the Japanese not only makes any new product payback uncertain, but also supports the new entry that might have struggled against existing norms. The rapid introduction of me-too versions enables consumers to accept more readily new features like front-wheel drive, all-black stereos, plastic hubcaps, and fully automatic cameras. The relative failures of four-channel stereo and the Betamax format only reinforce this point, showing how a lack of followers jeopardizes success.

Thus, the striving for uniqueness that characterizes Western positioning thought has its own high costs. It requires investment in new designs, new tooling, new promotional campaigns, dealer training, and consumer education. We all—independent distributors, wholesalers, retailers, salespersons, parents, children, consumers—have to learn. It's fun, when we are involved—but who needs another gizmo? For the company, getting everything right the first time is difficult, service personnel must learn new technology, and sales clerks must learn new product features. Customers who don't know what they are getting into know what they don't like, and satisfaction goes down. With so many choices in the mature markets, who needs it?

By contrast, the incremental augmentation of the currently leading brand generates high satisfaction scores. It does not, of course, sit so comfortably with a manufacturer or marketer who believes that the aim is to be innovative, create a special product, and do something no one else can do. But the products fill a need—and as we get more adept at using them, added features seem to make sense, just as Bill Gates says in his book.[80]

MAINTAINING LEADERSHIP

A market leader's best defense against competitive imitation is not a rear-guard move to stall the competition, but a preemptive strike. Toshiba's strategy in laptops illustrates how competitive churning helps a first-mover develop and expand a new market.

Shoji Hiroe, a division executive for PC Systems at Toshiba, happily reminisced about Toshiba's success with the laptops overseas.[81]

> The laptop market was a great success for Toshiba despite—and perhaps because of—the entrance of several competitors. Toshiba had a first-mover advantage in brand recognition, and had managed to establish the dominant design for the new product category. Its ability in flat-screen technology had finally been sufficiently advanced to produce a picture resolution that made laptops a viable complement or even alternative to desktop computers. The other key components—portability for ease of carrying, and battery operations for use away from home or office—came from intensive development work both within the company and with outside vendors. The portability, in particular, relied on the rapid diffusion of miniaturization technology throughout the Japanese consumer electronics industry. It became possible to produce laptops weighing only a little more than ten pounds, quite acceptable for carrying it along during travel.
>
> The imitators had to retool to get up to speed on a product many had written off because of the screen resolution problems. Zenith, then still American-owned, introduced its own unit in 1987, retailing for about $1,800 compared to the $2,300 required for the Toshiba in the American discount outlets. Because of its lower price and comparable performance characteristics, it was quickly dubbed the "Toshiba-killer." The first Japanese manufacturers entering the market [NEC and Epson], concentrated on compatibility with the NEC operating system and were not direct competitors of Toshiba. As in desktops, NEC's dominance in Japan was a double-edged sword. It allowed the company easy access to already loyal customers, but the incompatibility between its operating system and MS-DOS made the company—and its Japanese compatriots—hampered overseas.

Toshiba never looked back. Realizing the benefits of having caught their Japanese competitors at half court, and not worried about the American competitors, they realized that the key was to grow the market, especially in the United States. The company embarked on a strong product line proliferation strategy of quickly introducing new features and new models and adding additional processing capacity.

This strategy served multiple purposes. First, it grew the market by making the laptops realistic competitors to the desktops, and by increasing the range of applications. Further, it forced prices down without introducing lower-priced models by antiquating previous or original models. Thus, it opened up the lower end of the market without aiming new products directly at it. At the same time, this strategy eroded the profit potential of Zenith's "Toshiba killer," which could not keep up with the product churning. Soon Zenith was forced off the market.

TARGETING FOREIGN COMPETITORS

The peculiarities of the Japanese home market would seem to be a big handicap when entering foreign markets, especially mature ones with their differentiation and strong incumbents. But not for the first or last time, the Japanese have turned their disadvantage into a competitive edge. Trying to understand incomprehensible foreigners, they have focused on the products they use. Instead of aiming at market segments, they have targeted competitors' products. Instead of finding a few strangers waiting eagerly for their special product, they attract competitors' customers, creating new segments by churning.

LIMITED REPERTORY

While a Japanese company copies new products from leading competitors in Japan, overseas it targets well-established Western products and brands. Toyota's imitations of the Volkswagen Beetle (the Corona) and the Mercedes (the Lexus), Seiko's Swiss-style watches, the early SLR cameras, the McDonald's replica called McBurger, the fountain pens, and so on are copies of Western products and brands that have had leading positions in the global markets for an extended period of time. In retrospective interviews and autobiographical reminiscences older Japanese executives almost always acknowledge the desire to emulate Western products. Younger managers tend to be more independent-minded, not only because Japan now leads in many product areas, but also because they have come to recognize the Western attitude toward imitation.

The Japanese are less prone to imitate new products from Western companies. The reason is twofold. One, an *established* foreign brand ensures an existing market, limiting the need for market research. Two, a *new* Western product might require materials, technology, and know-how that the Japanese firm does not (yet) possess. Since it is unproven in the marketplace, the effort to tool up production of a me-too version is less easily justified. By contrast, Japanese companies usually have no monopoly access to specific resources (except perhaps "smarter" people), so the follower companies can broadly count on being able to make a similar product.

This is why some products in the West are sometimes left unassailed by the Japanese, even though they would seem a natural target from a competitive viewpoint. The Swatch watches, the Chrysler Vanagon, the new multimedia hardware, and the new PC software especially represent new markets in which, clearly, the lack of skills—or confidence—kept the Japanese sidelined for a time, only to enter late from the bench, as the markets mature.

ENTERING FOREIGN MARKETS

When Western companies enter foreign markets, they usually come with a new product or new technology, and their task is to create a new segment or market. Classic examples include the Singer sewing machine, the nylon shirt, and the long-playing (LP) record. Newer cases include personal computers, Levi's blue jeans, and McDonald's fast food. The marketing challenge is the development of latent demand, often where domestic competition is simply nonexistent.

Japanese companies do not usually face this situation. Rather, many of their successful landings in foreign markets occur in mature markets with firmly ensconced domestic competitors. Not surprisingly, their strategies seem strange to Westerners accustomed to diverse market situations. Viewing the rocky shores that the Japanese have faced, many marketing strategists are impressed by their achievements.

So, how do Western companies enter mature markets? The textbooks emphasize the new entrant's uniqueness, a new feature or two, and then targets "open" and undefended niches in the market. The new entrant stresses its uniqueness and avoids head-to-head battles with the market leaders.

The Japanese approach is quite different, but is also changing over time. In the 1950s, companies like Toyota and Sony entered at the lower end of the market, creating a beachhead niche from which to launch later inroads up-market.[82] This strategy is no longer viable today, when other Asian countries have adopted it, and when Japanese products occupy more upscale market niches. Instead, in mature foreign markets, the Japanese adopt a target-the-leader strategy to overseas entry. They aim for a well-established brand, perhaps the market leader; benchmark and reverse-engineer that product and develop a similar alternative; choose a position indistinguishable, except for price, from that of the competitor, including one that might also be Japanese; and then attempt to replace the leader. Rather than trying to test the waters in a low position, the now-experienced Japanese firm will go head to head against the best.

Exhibit 5:3 shows the pattern, how the Japanese match basic product features to those of the target brand, and then identify the appropriate price position. Using well-known benchmarking and quality function deployment techniques, they arrive at a competitive design through reverse engineering. Choosing a price position to the left of the diagonal area in the figure, the Japanese can offer a superior price/value package. Exhibit 5:4 shows the Lexus luxury automobile from Toyota. By meticulously disassembling several Mercedes cars, Toyota could design and build a luxury machine that consumers rate higher than its target, and whose competitive price has made it a great success.[83]

Exhibit 5:3
On-Target Positioning

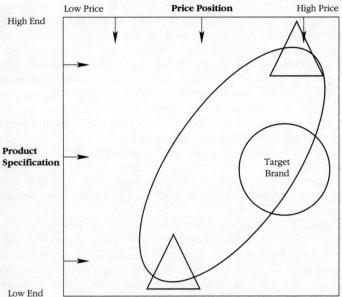

Exhibit 5:4
On-Target Positioning: Lexus Example

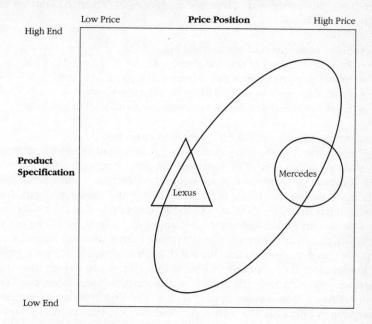

IMITATION ADVANTAGES

There are clear advantages to the Japanese entry strategy. First of all, using a target-the-leader strategy means that the strategy fundamentals are in place. This position represents a sizable part of market demand. The technology necessary to build a me-too product is known and available, or at least obtainable. Furthermore, if the firm wants to become a major player in this market, it needs this kind of product in its line sooner or later.

Other factors also favor an imitative entry. There is no need to spend a lot on advertising to educate buyers about product features: You need only to showcase the features added. And there is less reason to spend on expensive market research with uncertain outcomes.

The supply side, of course, plays a role. Local subassemblers, component manufacturers, and parts suppliers might hesitate to invest in new and costly machines to tool up for a new design positioned in an as-yet unfilled hole in the perceptual space. The company might have to guarantee order quantities greater than prudent and assist its supplier conversion in other ways. If the parts used are those in the market leader's dominant design, then the risks to all parties are much lower.

Immediately after entry, the competitive rivalry becomes intense as the churning gets under way. From the proliferation of various features the typical result is:

- Shifts in the product positioning maps.
- Rapid extensions of product lines.
- Immediate imitation of new features that promise to sell.
- Promotion with an emphasis on brand names.
- Unprecedented and free service to create and sustain loyalties.

Churning creates a fickle and pampered customer.

The drawback of the entry strategy is the direct and awesome challenge to a strong incumbent. The Japanese have the conviction that they can out-compete many Western firms when the battle turns on *execution* of strategy.[84] By benchmarking the leading brand, the challenger neutralizes many of the strategic advantages of the incumbent, so that the rivalry centers on incremental modifications and amplifying efforts, including service at which the Japanese excel. The strengths of the incumbent are turned to shackles, as the dominant firm finds it difficult to compete in a new game.

Empirically, the churning intensifies further when more than one Japanese entrant arrives. The wait is usually not very long. When one company enters a large foreign market such as the United States, its Japanese competitors follow shortly: Panasonic, Toshiba, and Hitachi soon followed Sony's Trinitron TV entry, and Datsun (now Nissan) and then Mazda trailed Toyota into the U.S. market. Japanese companies even try to use the same advertising agencies, perhaps not so strange when you consider the uncertainties involved. After Grey advertising managed the successful Honda motorcycle campaign ("You meet the nicest people on a Honda"), Canon chose Grey to introduce its AE–1 camera, featuring tennis player John Newcombe. Grey has become practically a Japanese specialist.[85]

The parallelism in company strategies is pervasive. For example, when Honda developed a new distribution network for its luxury Acura line to overcome contractual limitations with its existing dealer network, Toyota adopted the same distribution strategy for its Lexus, and Nissan, for its Infiniti line.

When only one Japanese company enters, as happens in smaller markets, the incumbent sustains less damage. The Japanese in Europe, with its traditionally fragmented markets, have not followed the imitative practice to the same extent. But with the European integration, the Japanese companies again show signs of parallelism, with auto companies preferring the United Kingdom for assembly, various companies congregating in Düsseldorf for their German or European headquarters, and so on.

The parallelism has practical advantages, of course. The Western service providers have shown themselves able to deal successfully with

Japanese clients. Blame for failure can be deflected more easily, since other Japanese firms used the same firm. It places competition between the Japanese on an equal footing, and avoids giving a competitor an advantage. Even though the practice also misses a potential advantage with a better partner, it avoids creating an advantage that rests on a Western service provider that you cannot easily control.[86]

"BUY JAPANESE"

The imitative rivalry between the Japanese companies leads to a synergistic surge of consumer demand for "buying Japanese." Consumers recognize the value offered from the intensely competitive Japanese firms and begin choosing among the indistinguishable Japanese offerings rather than from Western manufacturers who stress only their uniqueness. The market shifts toward Japanese products. Not being Japanese will be a barrier to marketplace success. The Japanese companies constitute their own "strategic group" in Porter's nomenclature: Customers will not buy Japanese goods simply because they are Japanese, but because they are the best buy. It is the "efficient market mechanism" at work.

The Japanese do tend to prefer Japanese products, but not because of patriotism. Rather, in their experience, Japanese products perform better, are more reliable, and offer better after-sales support. This is why foreign customers buying Japanese products are not "unpatriotic"—they simply follow the same logic. In the latest comparisons across countries, Japan's product quality comes out on top, followed by Germany and the United States.[87-88]

Exhibit 5:5
On-Target Entry

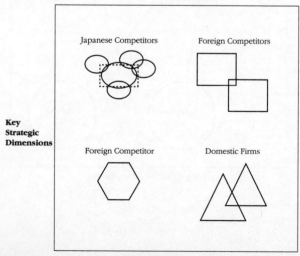

Target Customer Segments

In foreign markets synergy creates a Japanese advantage with a striking pattern of market evolution. Exhibit 5:5 shows how Japanese companies target the leader in a particular segment of the market, just as Toyota did with the VW Beetle and the Lexus, Uni-Charm did with Pampers, Nintendo did with Atari (and now Sega is doing with Nintendo—"He who lives by the sword will die by the sword"). Through churning, they attract customers to their offerings (Exhibit 5:6), the demand side effect. Gradually, as the Japanese increase their total market share and expand their product lines to reach additional segments, other non-Japanese companies must incorporate the new technology and the new features. Mercedes is trying to match Lexus in quiet ride, a strong selling point for Lexus. Pampers became thinner and more fitted to the baby's contours because of Uni-Charm's additions. Nintendo not only outdid Atari in arcade games, but invented the Gameboy, a hand-held arcade game, which just about finished Atari (just as Hewlett-Packard's hand-held calculator spelled doom for desktop calculators). This is the supply side effect (see Exhibit 5:7). The end result is a shift in the marketplace, toward the Japanese offerings.

Exhibit 5:6
Changing Preferences

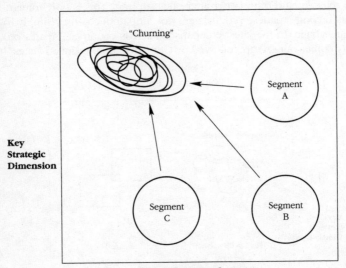

Target Customer Segments

Exhibit 5:7
Competitive "Pull"

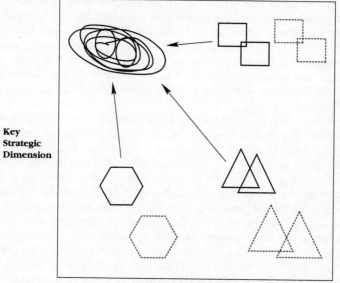

Key Strategic Dimension

Target Customer Segment

In the end, it is little wonder that the success of the Japanese in the mature foreign markets seems to have had more to do with speed and precision of execution than with the soundness of any marketing strategy in and of itself. The Japanese competitive style has come to mean many sleepless nights for executives around the world.

IMITATION IS GOOD

Explanations for the Japanese targeting of competitors are not hard to find. Market demand in Japan is more homogeneous than in a country such as the United States: There are fewer niches in the market with sufficient demand. Each player needs to copy a competitor's successful product and to launch a competing version, so as not to jeopardize its entire market. Thus, focusing on competitive products amounts to focusing on the market. That is the demand side explanation: Being competitor-oriented does not mean that the Japanese are not market-oriented—competitor and customer are opposite sides of the same coin.

But other factors are at work as well from the supply side, as it were. First of all, in Japan imitation is clearly the sincerest form of flattery, and perfect imitation is something that seems to come naturally to Japanese from their early education: Instead of *Mr. Rogers*-style TV programs that teach children "you are special," Japan's children's programming emphasizes allegiance to the group. Very few company employees in Japan say, "Well, that may be the way they do it, but we want to do it another way." Rather, the Japanese sentiment is, "If they do it successfully, then we must do it too."

Furthermore, most companies in a given industry are equally endowed in their natural resources. The key difference becomes simply a matter of manpower. True, inequality results from the granting of rights to import raw materials, government procurement rules, and similar, often long-standing, privileges, especially advantageous to older companies. The *keiretsu* system also protects some companies over others. Nevertheless, with very weak patent protection laws and government attempts to share new technology among all firms, the competitive differentiation among companies in the same industry boils down to the skills of the employees. Since the labor market is not mobile, the focus on competition understandably becomes intense, filled with personal angst for all the players. To be beaten by a competitor is to be beaten in a team race.

The death from overwork (*karosi*) mentioned in chapter 1 is a relatively recent phenomenon, but the pressure to perform has been there longer. One reason the Japanese spend long hours at work is simply that work helps reduce the stress. Vacations of the length common among Europeans are unimaginable—the stress of being away from work for so long would be unbearable to many employees. As always, Japan is the upside-down country.

In the West the unequal access to various firm-specific resources gives the companies monopolistic advantages and promotes a sense of uniqueness, but the Japanese have no such excuses for a subpar performance. The Japanese employee strongly correlates his company's performance with his own self-worth (and, of course, his semiannual bonus).

Some chief executive officers in successful companies (NEC, Sony, TDK, Suntory) try to instill a sense of uniqueness in their organizations by broad proclamations of company goals. As "individualism" seems to attract the now more affluent consumer in Japan, so does "uniqueness" attract the successful corporation. But, in both cases, the efforts are still limited so as not to threaten group allegiances.[89]

⮞ PART III
GETTING IT DONE

6

MAKING THAT PRODUCT

Product decisions are only one part of the marketing mix. But, for the Japanese, products represent the core of the mix. With their combined product and customer focus, products are naturally the beginning point for them. The price they set for their products is almost always "competitive," in their words, reflecting the concern with competition—and their products.

It is one thing to say, as we did in the chapter on intuitive incrementalism, that the Japanese, turning apparent weakness into strength, are speedy and flexible. It is one thing to emphasize benchmarking and reverse engineering, as we did in the last chapter, as keys to product churning and competitive price positioning. It is still not clear how they do it. What happens inside the organization? What do they do when they reverse-engineer? How do they handle—and think about—other marketing tools, like advertising and distribution support? These are the questions answered in this third part of our book. To get started we have to say something about the marketing mix.

THE MARKETING MIX

Beginning with McCarthy's textbook at the end of the 1950s, the decision areas of the marketing manager have typically been organized as a mix of "four P's":

- Product, including product line, new products.
- Price, including position in the market.

- Promotion, from advertising to point of sale.
- Place, or choice of distribution channel.

The role of the manager is to develop a harmonious blend of these areas to maximize the product's chances of success in the marketplace.

FOUR UNEQUAL P'S

Many Western texts present the four P's as separable, although not independent, decision areas. Not surprisingly, given the lack of functional specialization in the Japanese corporation, such separation is not considered useful. A strong hierarchical relationship among the four P's makes it necessary to take the decisions in the correct order.

In the Western company the decisions about the four P's fall into clearly defined time horizons. Prices can quickly and easily be reduced by temporary promotional activities (deals, two-for-one, coupons), perhaps supported by changes in local media support. A national media campaign is going to take longer to implement, and will often play itself out over several months. To compete through improved products requires even longer time horizons. Finally, changes in distribution arrangements, apart from special promotions, are made only rarely and require a lot of preparation and the shifting of resources.

Because of the different skills required for the various tasks, it is common to find differences across companies in the degree to which certain P's are emphasized over others. In the United States, for example, Unilever is considered a strong image builder, less of a strong distributor. In some of the same markets, Kimberly-Clark's products are considered very good, but its promotional flair is not so highly regarded. Another competitor, Procter & Gamble, does well on product and distribution, and is also a formidable advertiser and all-around strong. These are subjective perceptions of Western and Japanese executives occasionally surfacing in interviews and newspaper reports. They do not, of course, represent "true" states of affairs, they are usually not agreed on even by company insiders, and they are not stable over time. Nevertheless, for the Japanese, folklore and stereotypes cannot be ignored when dealing with competitors and customers.

PRODUCT FOCUS

The Japanese companies are more similar to one another. They start with the product—the Japanese companies are generally product-oriented.

Whether it is a new product or—the more common case—a me-too version, all Japanese companies take pride in their product. Without a good product, the firm will not stay in business long. The competition is just too severe.

The chosen price level is derived from competitive parity, and the choice is based mainly on how the product stacks up against the leader in the targeted segment. In fact, because of the intense competition with other Japanese companies, most Japanese marketers are price takers rather than price makers. They find where in the market similar products lie on the price line.[90]

Unlike price, distribution decisions by the Japanese involve a great deal of effort. Distribution channels provide not only a means to make the product available, but determine how close to the customers the manufacturer can get. It is also a less reversible decision, and even with the Japanese ability and willingness to work closely to shore up a weak channel, mistakes will be costly. Mitsubishi's decision to use the Chrysler dealer network in the United States has been responsible for its slow penetration of the U.S. market. Distribution decisions are also viewed as critical because of the traditional lack of alternative channels in the Japanese markets, something that affects Japanese as well as foreign firms, but that now seems to be less of a problem. The problems of distribution in Japan, with its many-layered system of gradually smaller wholesalers and a large number of mom-and-pop stores, have been well-documented, although things have eased with the emergence of larger chains, including discount stores selling imported merchandise.[91]

The main difference in the marketing manager's decision mix is the relatively minor role played by promotions and the peculiar nature of media advertising. Promotions play a much smaller role in the Japanese market than in the United States because of tradition more than outright prohibition. Promotions are not so much a way of competing, but a way of adding value and differentiation to the offering. While in the United States unique products are going head-to-head in promotional wars, with Japanese products promotions create differentiation. When such thinking is transferred abroad, the result is not always positive. Nissan's ads for its luxury car Infiniti, with their reflective and unfocused copy and visuals, aiming to create a brand image of mystique and "poetic dream," common elements of advertising in Japan, were largely ridiculed in the more prosaic U.S. press. For Americans, the theme of "having arrived at an exalted station in life" needs more palpable symbolism.[92]

When Procter & Gamble introduced its all-temperature Cheer detergent on the Japanese market in the late 1970s, the company transferred from the United States its popular and successful "cents-off" coupon campaigns coupled with point-of-purchase displays and retailer incentives. Although consumers were interested, the promotion was largely a failure. The small and crowded stores could not offer enough shelf space and had only small or no backroom storage areas, leading to out-of-stock conditions and weak product flow-through. The retailers, although willing to cooperate, were unfamiliar with the coupons, and because the register clerks spent time reading each coupon carefully, customer service deteriorated. When Kao, the largest competitor, applied pressure, stores simply opted out of the promotional program.[93]

As for media advertising, which does play a large role even though the recession has hit budgets, institutional and cultural reasons account for the differences. First of all, advertising agencies in Japan are much more powerful entities than in the West. In Japan an agency such as giant Dentsu controls many of the media vehicles available (including TV programs), and even produces some of the shows. The agencies can also accept work from clients who are competitors, using different units within the organization to maintain confidentiality. Both of these factors give the agency more flexibility and greater power vis-à-vis the clients.

A cultural reason for delegating most authority over media communication decisions to the agency is that advertising is a matter of "blowing your own horn." Naturally a firm in a socially reticent society like Japan allows an independent party to conduct the advertising, much as a *nakodo*, or go-between matchmaker, arranges a marriage. This reticence also leads the agency to use much more soft-sell approaches than in the West. Japanese advertising agencies provide interesting places of work to very creative and even "high art" individuals.

The same impulse also guides the agency in developing copy with much less of a product-information or unique-selling-proposition approach. The emphasis on image and brand name that has been noticed by so many observers of marketing in Japan flows naturally from the avoidance of concrete bits of information and the preoccupation with form in social communication. Japanese advertising is "weird," often not even making clear what product or brand is being advertised.

Most Japanese companies use local agencies when entering overseas markets, not their domestic agency's branches, contrary to the practice of many Western companies. Since the Japanese advertising agencies operate under very different conditions at home, they do not travel well. Furthermore, given the bad reception of the few attempts of transfer, such as the Infiniti ads, it is perhaps not surprising that Japanese companies abroad give a very free hand to their Western advertising agencies, allowing creativity to flow unhindered.

Overall, the fact that the various strands of the marketing mix often seem to weave together into one integrated unit in the successful Japanese company abroad is not due to careful prior analysis. The soft-sell advertising may be mistaken by not talking about attributes or even benefits of the product, as Nissan's derogated Infiniti ads showed. The distribution may or may not be the best choice for the product, as Shiseido found out when it entered United States via drugstore chains. But not to worry—the incremental approach to strategy usually adopted by the Japanese helps to correct such faux pas. For them, the point is to avoid locking themselves into an indefensible position and then having to defend it. Over time, trial and error will yield the right mix.

New Product Development

There is today a great deal of R&D in basic technology going on in Japan. While early efforts up to the 1980s aimed to center research in Japan, more recent strategies have focused on developing transnational research tie-ups to make it possible for the Japanese to draw on the strong research capabilities of Western scientists and laboratories.[94] Nevertheless, as in the past, the major share of industrial R&D expenditures fall into the development category, and are spent on bringing new ideas to the marketplace in Japan.

Given that product strategies are the cornerstone of their marketing effort, new product development by the Japanese is naturally important. The proliferation of new features that characterizes the competitive churning often involves the imaginative application of new technology, resulting in incrementally "new and improved" products. A common approach to designing such technology-driven new products is to construct what Sony calls the "mindset" of the user, and to visualize how the new technology may expand the possibilities. An example from Hitachi, the large electric appliance maker, shows how this works. It is easy to spot the need for smaller-sized appliances such as washing machines in Japan—nobody gets extra points for suggesting this. But by visiting users in their homes, Hitachi discovered that noise regulations prohibited use of even small machines during a large portion of the evening or early morning—and in the daytime the stay-home mothers wanted to get out of the cramped quarters. The solution was to develop a quieter washer that could be used anytime, even in apartments with thin walls. This development then opened up the market segment of young, single women with jobs who in growing numbers had decided that married life was not yet for them. The ability to wash any time during the day or at night has now become a core function, and noisier washers don't make the grade anymore. Similarly, when Yamaha introduced a miniature radio cassette player with improved sound quality, it attracted not the targeted teenagers but customers in their thirties and forties, leading to the boom in mini-component systems in the mid-1980s.[95]

FAST DEVELOPMENT

How the Japanese cut the development time for new products has been well-documented in the published literature.[96] Marketers, designers, and engineers work closely together, and what in the West are sequential activities—preliminary screening, proposed design, cost assessment, demand estimation, prototype, test marketing—are overlapping activities in Japan with continuous sharing of feedback. Exhibit 6:1 shows the *sashimi* process described by Takeuchi and Nonaka (1986), so called because it resembles the way Japanese cut raw fish for serving, with sequential activities started before prior steps are finished. The shortened process helps bring new technology to market quickly.

Exhibit 6:1
Sashimi Process of New Product Development

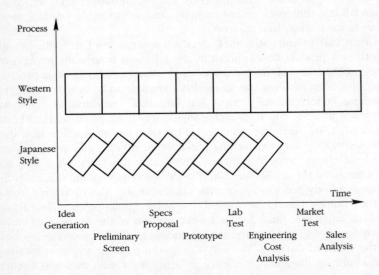

The speeded-up development process increases competitive pressure and increases the pace of market evolution. First of all, Western innovators are preempted. There are many examples of Western companies' technological innovations brought to the market first by the Japanese, including the transistor, the VCR, and the auto-focus camera. In this fash-

ion the Japanese have often captured first-mover advantages, and, in the case of Kyocera and ceramics, no Japanese followers have eroded that advantage.

Second, the fast development time is aided by reverse engineering, not necessarily of end products but also of subassemblies and components. Thus, the Japanese are particularly fast with me-too products. The loyal customers in Japan are often willing to wait a little for their favorite brand to match any new offering. This in turn induces the companies to the churning behavior we discussed in the previous chapter.

Third, the fast development time and the imitative product strategies result in rapid diffusion of the new product. As a result, the product life-cycle slope is getting steeper. The introductory stage is shorter, the growth stage arrives earlier, and the curve is level during a relatively short period, after which new products displace the existing technology (see Exhibit 6:2). In other words, the maturity stage is shorter—some say that in Japan's home market, where so many variants are marketed, it never arrives. This is Japan's version of "cutthroat" competition. Product focus, not price focus.

Exhibit 6:2
Steeper/Shorter Product Life Cycles

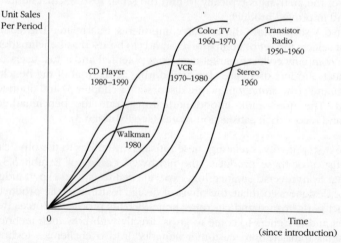

Unit Sales Per Period

Color TV 1960–1970

Transistor Radio 1950–1960

CD Player 1980–1990

VCR 1970–1980

Stereo 1960

Walkman 1980

0

Time
(since introduction)

The success of the Japanese companies that have "learned" from competitive products seems to have been a factor in the recent popularity of similar techniques in the West. Competitive benchmarking and "best practices" studies across competitors have been quoted as one reason for the catching up of the American automobile industry. The quality function

deployment (QFD) technique, which ties customer preferences directly into the new product attributes, is an important marketing innovation by the Japanese.

THE QFD TECHNIQUE

As we have seen, in Japan all company personnel are expected to spend time with customers and product users, listening and learning. Treating marketing is too important for marketers alone; designers and production engineers are attuned to customer needs and desires. Not surprisingly, some engineers decide to apply their scientific minds to the task of combining their customer research with new product development. One result has been the QFD technique, originating with the automobile companies, but quickly spread throughout Japanese industry.

The QFD technique is a good example of how Japanese engineers have influenced company marketing practices. This method, also known as "the house of quality," consists of four components: customer importance ratings, competitive product rankings, physical description of competing products, and correlation between features and customer ratings.[97] The aim of the analysis is typically to find the set of features that defines a new and improved product.

Exhibit 6:3 shows how these four components interrelate. The company first selects the set of competitive brands to be used as benchmarks. Then the company collects market data from potential and actual users of the product. Product users are observed during actual trial of the benchmarked brands (the *sangen* principle discussed in chapter 3) and queried afterward. The users rank important features, rate the benchmarked brands, and record their satisfaction scores (see Exhibit 6:3).

The next step involves relating these satisfaction ratings to the physical characteristics of these products (the northwest corner of Exhibit 6:3). Using data from reverse engineering, experimental tests, and expert judgment, the designers correlate the physical design features of the products to product performance and customer benefits. This procedure forces the engineers and designers to come to grips directly with how their technological skills translate into customer benefits. It also challenges technicians to develop advances over competitors that result in tangible customer gains. For example, in the case of the Lexus, the Mercedes cars benchmarked were all much less noisy than existing Toyota cars. Wanting to avoid the obvious solution of using thicker gauge steel for the chassis, the Lexus team leveraged its skill in manufacturing precision parts to

Exhibit 6:3
QFD: Quality Function Development

| | Functional Characteristics ▲ Strong Correlation ● Some Correlation ■ Possible Correlation | | | | Customer Satisfaction Scale: 1 to 5 (5=Best) | | | | |
	Pencil Length (inches)	Time Between Sharpenings (written lines)	Lead Dust (particles per line)	Hexagonality	Importance Rating (5 = highest)	Writesharp (now)	Competitor X (now)	Competitor Y (now)	Writesharp (target)
Customer Demands Easy to Hold	●			●	3	4	3	3	4
Does Not Smear		●	▲		4	5	4	5	5
Point Lasts	■	▲	●		5	4	4	3	5
Does Not Roll	■			▲	2	3	3	3	4
Benchmarks Writesharp (now)	5	56	10	70%					
Competitor X (now)	5	84	12	80%					
Competitor Y (now)	4	41	10	60%					
Writesharp (target)	5.5	100	6	80%					

	Writesharp	Competitor X	Competitor Y	Writesharp
Market Price	15¢	18¢	14¢	16¢
Market Share	16%	12%	32%	20%
Profit	2¢	3¢	2¢	4¢

Data: GOAL/QPC, BW

increase the fit in the body parts, virtually eliminating noise while keeping weight and gas mileage at acceptable levels.

REVERSE ENGINEERING

We have been using the concepts of reverse engineering freely until now, and it is useful to spell out some more detail about what it entails.

The basic notion of reverse engineering is to acquire one or more samples of a competitor's product, and then carefully disassemble them. It is similar to an autopsy—the Japanese call it a *tenji kai*—and it is useful to have more than one sample, since that way the autopsy can stop at various levels for different units, from a simple removal of the outer shell all the way to a complete disassembly into the smallest parts and subassemblies. When the Lexus LS 400 was designed, Toyota was reported to have bought four upscale Mercedes cars for the autopsy.

The teams assigned to do the reverse engineering are usually all technicians, but with varying levels of experience and expertise. Usually a senior engineer heads the teams, and it is important that the team members are also responsible for designing the company's own version. In the case of new and original assemblies and novel problem solutions, the team will attempt to draft the underlying blueprint, extracting the concept behind the actual hardware. Given the blueprint, the solution's performance rating can quickly be tested using standard CAD/CAM techniques. Alternatively, of course, the engineers can simply do a real-life stress test, even pushing the hardware until it breaks (another reason that more than one sample is useful).

The Japanese companies will often invite their first-line suppliers to send a team participant, and sometimes smaller suppliers and also larger customers or dealers are invited to review the "carcass." The suppliers for the larger Japanese companies often have important roles to play in the new product development effort, and inviting the customers can be a public relations advantage.

In 1994, when Toyota dissected the new Chrysler Neon, dubbed the "Japan-fighter" and slated for introduction in Japan by early 1996, executives and engineers from 240 supplier companies—often as many as three representatives from a single company—were invited. Thousands of disassembled Neon parts were laid out in a large exhibition hall, and the suppliers walked through, taking notes and talking to Toyota engineers. "The idea is for suppliers to find out things for themselves, to touch and feel, rather than sitting through a seminar at which Toyota tells us of their conclusions," according to one supplier official.

Not all reverse-engineering projects are of that scale. The Neon was chosen because of its positioning against the Japanese lower-end models, and also because it represented the state of the art of American carmaking after the so-called lean manufacturing lessons from Japan had supposedly been absorbed. The Neon example shows not only that companies follow market leaders, but how closely even leaders actually follow new developments. In an unusual development, Toyota's assessment from the Neon autopsy was published after the information was leaked from Toyota, possibly intentionally. Toyota, necessarily partial, suggested that the Neon was not up to exacting Japanese standards, but said it learned some valuable lessons about possible cost savings—such as increased use of plastic in the engine and a simplified system for punching holes in sheet metal from one side only—from the autopsy.[98]

DESIGNING THE CLONE

Having completed the matrix in Exhibit 6:3, the design team can identify what a new and improved product might offer. Evaluating several possible new combinations of features against what customers rank as most important features, the designers create the alternative with the best competitive advantage. The preference data force the designers and engineers to face customer desires directly. For example, a small improvement in a very important benefit can mean much more than a technologically greater improvement in a less salient feature.

Throughout, everybody on the project team is expected to raise—and help solve—manufacturability questions: How can the new product be designed so that manufacturing costs are reduced? If the competing products are Japanese, technological capability is often less of a problem, since most companies possess the necessary skills. Benchmarking foreign products, on the other hand, sometimes leads to a long incubation period, because the company might not possess the necessary know-how. For example, in the case of disposable diapers, two Japanese companies, Kao and Uni-Charm, benchmarked and later improved on Procter & Gamble's Pampers, the first-mover. But because the Japanese lacked necessary technological know-how (knowledge about the absorption power of various paper fibers had to be developed, for example), P&G had the Japanese market to itself from 1976 to 1982, before Uni-Charm introduced its Moony brand.

In the early stages, the cost side is less important in the Japanese QFD process than is customary in Western companies. Once the preferred combination of features has been identified and the market price decided on, production engineers have to bring costs in line. The process here is not simple, involving practices such as value engineering through which designers and process engineers work to simplify production and redesign to avoid expensive production steps. The marketing input in this stage is relatively minimal, but it needs to be emphasized that this is usually not cost cutting in the sense that cheaper materials are substituted in minor parts. Changing from leather to plastic on the automobile's dashboard, for example, may save money, but may also compromise customer satisfaction. Rather, the designers work closely with production people (and keep doing it—*kaizen*) until they come up with manufacturable minimum-cost designs.[99]

MARKET EVOLUTION

Because markets evolve, Japanese new-product development involves more than benchmarking and QFD to match and improve on existing brands. Targeting markets also requires anticipation of where the market is headed. Japanese companies use their new product churning to move markets in directions beneficial to their products.

Because intuitive incrementalism is necessarily imprecise, when Japanese products are new on the market they are not always as well-targeted as the more scientifically researched Western brands. Examples include the early problems of the Acura Legend, Honda's luxury entry; the slow acceptance of Sony's Soundabout, later renamed the Walkman; and Mitsubishi's large-screen TV sets. Not to worry. Strong support of dealers, flexible adaptation of product, and persistent advertising support combined with patient capital and a long-term view turn immediate failures into later successes.

Many Western companies that are ahead of Japanese with new products have difficulty protecting themselves against the Japanese churning. The reasons are twofold. First, new Western products usually need a shakedown period, a time when quirks are ironed out, while the Japanese new products work well from day one. Second, the churning, as we have seen, tends to shift preferences.

The manufacturing excellence of the Japanese companies has come to mean that their new products usually arrive on the market with zero defects. Western companies are catching up, but in the past their offerings have usually taken some time to settle down. This has of course led to a squandering of potential first-mover gains, as some customers will stay on the sidelines, and pioneering buyers will be dissatisfied because of low quality. The problems plaguing Microsoft's Macword (a word count that took minutes to complete, for example) and the delayed launch of its Windows 95 highlighted the problems involved in shipping PC software too early. The Japanese companies will rarely take that risk. Even though they enter incrementally, and are ready to adapt the product quickly, the actual functioning of the product is guaranteed.

As the possibly mispositioned Japanese companies get their product modification and the continuous improvement (*kaizen*) machine going, they will zero in on the market, and then the new features will start shifting customer preferences. By the time the Western companies have fixed the problems in their new products, the market has moved away. Exhibit 6:4 depicts the dynamic process.[100]

Exhibit 6:4
Targeting versus Churning

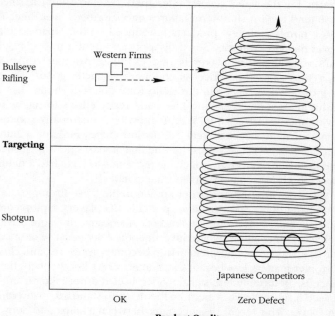

The exhibit depicts a process that has familiar overtones. The new Western product is designed to fit a particular target segment, but less attention is typically paid to the reliability and quality, resulting in an acceptable performance but not zero defects. That can come later as users' complaints come in and production improvements are made. This is not acceptable to the Japanese followers, who imitate the new product, design their own version, and introduce it. The problem for them is that their market research is less scientific, and this can hurt, especially early in the product life cycle when managers' intuitions are not yet tuned in correctly. As an automobile executive said to us once, "Why should the Americans drive trucks to movies—trucks are for work."

But as the churning speeds up the proliferation in the marketplace, the "tornado" moves in on the target market, sweeps slow-moving competitors aside, and moves customers to new heights. Instead of responding to expressed customer needs, the leader of the market drives the preferences, helped by the other Japanese companies.

With the emphasis on me-too-plus products that drive the market, the new-product success rate seems greater for the Japanese than for Western companies. But the actual success rates are difficult to establish, since the Japanese tend to turn short-term failures into successes over time. There are also a number of new products introduced on the Japanese market that never make it overseas. Some disappear without a trace. Mitsubishi Electric's vertical record player is one example. Another comes from Sanrio, a Tokyo-based producer of children's character goods. The company's great success has been the Hello Kitty doll, which also has been successful internationally. Sanrio has made many efforts to follow Hello Kitty with another success. In a 1991 interview, a company spokesman mentioned that in a typical year Sanrio introduces perhaps a hundred new products in its Tokyo stores, hoping that at least one will be successful. The new Kero-Kero-Keroppi character seems to have had a modicum of success, both in Japan and in the United States.

The successes are perhaps better known in the West. Examples include new one-hand-only 35mm cameras, portable CD players, laptop computers, fax machines, electronic organizers, videocams. In more advanced technological innovations, where investment is risky because of uncertain standards, imaginative entrepreneurship becomes necessary, and close-to-the-customer matters less because customers don't know much, the performance is predictably less stellar. Videodiscs did not take off until the RCA-based laser technology became the de facto standard, over Pioneer's analog player. The recent disagreement between Philips and Sony over digital audiotape and the problem of the format for video recording discs (now resolved in a compromise between Sony and Toshiba) shows how some of these issues are too big to be settled in the marketplace. The first-mover might choose the wrong fork in the road.

NEW PRODUCT INNOVATION

As the Japanese successes have pushed the companies to the forefront of several industries, the Japanese have few or no models to benchmark and modify. The companies have to become more innovative and develop new products from scratch. A few leaders at some companies—Sony and Honda are perhaps best known—have long directed their organizations toward innovation, but for many companies, such fundamental R&D represents a new challenge. How do the Japanese develop truly new innovations?

As one might expect, their approach deviates considerably from that of the Western innovators. Rather than relying on a collection of individual inventors coming up with new ideas and patentable breakthroughs, the Japanese new-product research involves many people in more or less constant interaction.

TECHNOLOGY-DRIVEN PRODUCTS

Companies like Sony in consumer electronics and Shiseido in cosmetics like to flaunt their lack of market research. Whether this is true or not, they usually do not do the kind of painstaking in-depth analysis of customers emblematic of scientific product positioning. The reason is that, fundamentally, these companies believe their products come first, customers follow. Products and technology, engineers and manufacturing people drive these companies, not the marketplace as it is today. There is a conviction embedded in the culture of these organizations that their products will create their own customers, that they lead the market. The reason for this conviction is clear. They are basically new-product companies.

In a company such as Sony, a disproportionate share of total revenues comes from products with less than one year on the market. With such new products, customer perceptions and preferences are still in the formative stages. Positioning maps are not valid, since consumers are still trying to understand the new benefits. Sony has a choice to wait until test markets are finished, or "go now." They usually opt for the latter. The transistor radio, the portable TV, the Trinitron color system, the Betamax, the Walkman, the video camcorder, the Discman, and the Watchman are all products for which market acceptance was difficult to judge before introduction—and which competitors quickly imitated.

The markets for these products developed *after* product introduction. The latent demand would have been difficult or impossible to identify through initial market research, and even the pioneering companies could not assume certain acceptance. The difficulties make Japanese designers and engineers join salespeople in visiting customers, and explain why a company such as Honda encourages employees to engage in *wai-gaya*, or free discussions, before decisions are taken.

The risk with such a "pro-active" strategy is obvious. Nobody might want the new product, and the company will be forced to introduce another one, and yet another. The downside risk has not stopped some commentators from endorsing the Japanese approach, arguing that because predictions are uncertain it is better to shoot many arrows and hope one will hit, rather than aim carefully with one—and miss.[101] And even if it hits, second-guessing competitors might buy the one model, reverse-engineer it, and produce a competing version in time to capture a large share of sales without an expensive campaign.

THE "MEANING" OF A PRODUCT

In some cases the new-product teams resemble the task forces assembled for crash programs (such as Kennedy's "land a man on the moon before the end of the decade") in the West. Honda's City car is an example. Assembling a cross-functional team of engineers and designers, none older than thirty to keep the team outlook "young," the company assigned the team the task of developing a new vehicle for the streets of Tokyo. The team was separated from the rest of the Honda R&D, and given a deadline to come up with a prototype. "We moved them in on the second floor, then set fire to the building" as one senior manager put it, using an image familiar to team members from one of Nintendo's successful Gameboy programs. The resulting car, a small vehicle with upright seat backs and lots of headroom, reminiscent of a London cab, became an instant success when introduced in 1989. It has been exported only to a select number of Asian markets.

Apple's Macintosh project, IBM's PC development, and similar successful team efforts are more adaptable to the Japanese managerial style than the "quirky inventor" type personified by Thomas Edison with his phonograph and Edwin Land of Polaroid. At the same time, given the new requirements for originality in innovation, the cross-functional Japanese teams have developed organizational processes for "creating knowledge" that go beyond individual creativity. Exhibit 6:5 shows the main features.

The fundamental process involves an initial brainstorming phase during which the team members freely exchange ideas and opinions. In this amplification stage, there is no attempt at reducing or focusing the team in a specific direction, and the team goal is often so ambiguous that it defies precise definition. The point is, in fact, for the team to define what the mission statement really means. A case in point is Nissan's Primera, a car that won the European car of the year award in 1990. The assigned mission by Nissan management was for the new product team to develop a "European car" for the EC market (the Primera has now been introduced in Japan as well, but not in the United States). During the amplification stage, several of the team members drove a car across Europe, from Brussels to Milano, to develop a tactile "feel" of what it means to be a European driver (the *sangen* principle of actual experience, as discussed in chapter 3).

Exhibit 6:5

Japanese and Western Product Development

	Western Type	Japanese Type
R & D Process		
Product concept	The product concept is clearly defined at early stages, and does not change throughout the process.	The product concept is ambiguous at early stages (amplification)
Developing the concept	The design target is fixed at an early stage based on the clearly defined concept. The target is pursued using division of labor.	While the concept is improved as the market may demand, it is realized by the collaboration among various departments (articulation)
R & D Management		
Pattern of team work	Phrased sequential approach	Overlapping (*sashimi*) approach
Objective of team work	Pursuit of the performance goal	Adaptation to changing needs
Team Organization	Functional organization or functional organization with weak project leaders.	Matrix organization with strong project leaders managing the whole development process or organization.
Strength	Efficient in terms of manpower. Reaches performance target.	Short lead time (three to four years). Adaptation to current needs. High production quality.
Weakness	Long lead time (seven to eight years). High development cost.	Inefficient use of manpower; may miss the performance target.

As the team gradually settles on an appropriate definition of the goal, the team members will all have the same understanding of it. Changes occur as new data come in and the marketplace changes, but all team members still interpret the goal similarly. In the articulation stage, the product definition starts taking shape, and various functional departments offer their views. In the Primera case, for example, the European concept as it evolved required tighter handling and steering than what Nissan had customarily offered, and production engineering specified the required production changes in machines, equipment, and training. In the articulation stage, the team members focus on making sure that all the tacit knowledge assimilated through the experiential research is captured in explicit design requirements. For example, the tacit "feel" and comfort of a car has to do with suspension and seat design, a matter of the size and weight of drivers and passengers. Consequently, the Primera seat designs and testing were done in England by Nissan UK, using only European drivers.

Most of the downstream development effort following the amplification and the articulation stages is done in the *sashimi* phased approach (see Exhibit 6:1), with supplier links, production engineering, and redesign tests ongoing simultaneously. Managing this type of process is a strong team leader at the center who can pull the various specialists together, so that potential conflicts are avoided and each functional specialist will understand and accept the need for any design changes. The advantage with the sequential Western approach is that once designers have signed off, the production engineers and manufacturing have a fixed blueprint to work from. On the other hand, the Japanese phased approach allows direct communication across functions, and therefore greater flexibility downstream. As the exhibit shows, the Japanese *sashimi* approach also leads to shorter development times.

THE SHARP SYSTEM

The Sharp Corporation, maker of innovative consumer electronics products, including the electronic organizer and the videocamera with a screen, exemplifies the length to which technology-driven Japanese companies go in order to develop new products that captivate customers.

In 1970, to develop stronger capability in new products, Sharp made a significant strategic decision to manufacture main components such as semiconductors in house. The company also made a number of organizational reforms, including forming an organizational unit concentrating on medium- to long-range research planning and establishing a central research center for sophisticated technology development. Two other organizational reforms were particularly important for the organization's marketing activities.

The first organizational reform involved the creation of a daily software planning department (*Seikatsu Soft Kikaku Honbu*), which focused on the development of original product concepts. New product concepts would emerge from three sources. One, a panel called the *Sense Leader Panel*, with approximately 600 users, was organized as an external sounding board. The panel members, ranging from teenagers to senior citizens, were divided into several groups, such as college students, housewives, and so on. When a new concept was developed, these groups could be further segmented for more focused results. Through these organized users, Sharp collected data to forecast future trends a year to ten years ahead.

Another new system facilitated joint research with companies from other fields. For example, when Sharp developed a toaster/microwave oven ahead of its competitors, insights from a joint research program with a food manufacturer were reflected in the product. The third source for new products was called the *Life Creator Panel*, involving a group of users as another external panel. The objective of this panel was to pursue possibilities of new lifestyles by experimenting with new technologies with users and companies from different fields. The Life Creator System, unlike ordinary product testing systems, involved users in direct discussions during the development stages before the completion of prototypes and products.

A second organizational reform was the establishment of a cross-functional organization called an Urgent Project Team. The Urgent Project Team started in 1977 in order to develop particularly important products/technologies within a year or two. When a department proposed a project requesting the "urgent" label, the proposal was examined at a General Technology Meeting. Once the proposal was adopted, the team leader was able to select appropriate team members from any department through letters of appointment issued by the company's president. The members then started working on the project full time and wore gold badges while the project was in progress. The gold badges represented the team's privileged access to necessary facilities, equipment, and materials. The Urgent Project Team reported directly to the president, and all team expenses were paid by the company's headquarters.

Sharp's Urgent Project Team was a mechanism to transform market data and customer feedback from the user panels into explicit forms and help team members share knowledge with each other. Three-dimensional CAD graphics utilized in concurrent product design helped the team members share a clear image of the product. As a result, they could examine the topological relationships between components and mechanical movements as well. Furthermore, they could evaluate the validity of various designs without any prototypes, by analyzing them using computers. Furthermore, during the process of model evaluation, a design defined by CAD was sent to the DNC (Direct Numerical Control) machining center where a model was produced. In this way, team members were able to examine a model with their own hands the day after they decided on its tentative design.

Sharp's product development system can be understood as a system to acquire customers' tacit knowledge by sharing the same experiences with them though panel discussions and prototype experiments enabling the company to create new product concepts. This team "socialization" process is very effective when the company needs to acquire and share tacit knowledge from customers, but it does cost a great deal and takes a fair amount of time.

PRODUCT LINE

In line with the preeminence of product, most Japanese companies will want to feature full product lines, at least in their home market. But a full product line to the Japanese firm does not necessarily imply the same range of products as for a Western firm. The number of variants might be the same—but the differences in Japan are much smaller.

FINE DISCRIMINATIONS

Take cosmetics, for example. A Western cosmetics company (like Revlon) might offer X different colors of lipstick, all nuances of red, from pale pink to dark purple. By contrast, a Japanese company such as Kanebo might offer X different colors as well, but within a much narrower range of red, from pink to dark red. Similarly for many other products, including consumer electronics and cars. Exhibit 6:6 depicts the typical pattern, showing a narrower range of product variants with a price range truncated at the top, but with a large number of product variants. Product markets in Japan show a degree of similar varieties bewildering to the Western observer.

The small differences in market preferences drive this close proliferation of models in the product line. The homogeneity of the Japanese market is striking when compared to the heterogeneous Western markets (especially the American). Not all Japanese product variants are exported—the differentiation between the models is too slight for the

Exhibit 6:6
Japanese vs. Western Full-Line Strategies

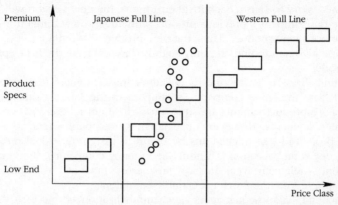

average consumer overseas. Many Japanese claim their choices at home are so much greater than overseas because of this. They usually are—in the range of products and features they would consider.

This is not to say that one cannot get everything in Japan. It is just that you have to pay for it—sometimes a lot. Throughout the booming 1980s status-oriented new products from abroad entered at a fast pace—only to slow down as the recession hit, and the cost of doing business in Japan skyrocketed. The imports have now shifted to the lower end of the market, hitting more of the core markets. Consumer variety is increasing. But from a global perspective, the consumer markets in Japan do not have very much variety.

So, in overseas markets, the Japanese companies do not usually offer a complete range of products. Over time, as the companies establish strong market positions, their growth mandate forces them to expand their product lines, often going beyond what they would be doing in the Japanese home market, a risky extension. Most Japanese companies prefer to introduce extensions that also fit the Japanese marketplace. The new luxury cars from Japan target overseas markets, even though the affluence at home has made them very strong sellers in Japan also.

COMPETING AGAINST YOURSELF

The "limited" full-line approach has, as everything else in Japan's marketplace, a competitive aspect. The intense product proliferation—due to the imitative positioning strategies—forces companies to introduce new product variants more or less continuously to maintain brand loyalties. When a new variant appears, a firm's loyal customers wait a short while for "their" company to introduce a similar version. Because of the quick reactions necessary to satisfy such loyal customers, the new version will usually be the company's previous product with added-on features from the competitor's new product. Thus, the new product is often a me-too from a competitive standpoint, and only slightly different from the firm's previous model.

"Cannibalization," with one model attracting customers from another model from the same company, is rampant in the Japanese market. A company's product variants are simply too close not to encroach on one another's segments. However, since Japanese companies tend to avoid using profit-and-loss calculations by brand to assign individual merit to managers, cannibalization is a nonissue in many companies. Brand management is relatively weak in most Japanese companies, with the usual exception of Kao, the Procter & Gamble emulator.

In general, Japanese managers view cannibalization as a necessary evil. Cannibalization is an unavoidable consequence of staying apace with the market. "If someone is going to steal our product's customers, it better be us," is the standard saying. To the dismay of many Western competitors, who end up trying to defend against a moving target, this same philosophy transfers abroad. Honda Accord made news in 1990, introducing a new model despite having the best-selling American car the year before.

Honda's product policy is interesting for another reason. A full-line policy, even in the "limited" sense of the Japanese, means generally an even range of models, from low-end to high-end. The range is not unidimensional—each price class offers a variety of different models to cater to slightly different tastes and segments. Nevertheless, there is some relationship between each item in the line, so that the customer can compare models in a general "compensatory" way ("I get more of this, less of that . . ."). As a unique type of company, Honda does not use the same logic in its product policy for autos (although it does for motorcycles).

As discussed at length by Sakakibara and Aoshima, Honda looks at each car model in its product line as a separate and unique model.[102] Honda does not conceive of a new model in relation to the others in the line. Toyota and Nissan follow the so-called life-cycle strategy, first devised by Sloan at General Motors, where the customer is offered a different model of the same make at each stage in life. Honda's product line strategy is different. Because of the individualistic philosophy of its founder, it has a different philosophy, with several models in the same price class. It evaluates each model strictly on its own merits, not because brand loyalty is unimportant, but because Honda wants each model to have its own unique target segment (see Exhibit 6:7).

Exhibit 6:7
Product Line Policy: The Toyota–Honda Difference

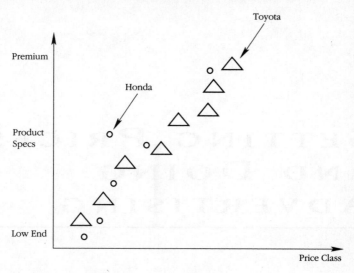

Support the Customer

American marketers tend to see their own convictions about the worth of a product as a prerequisite for effective selling. "If you don't believe in the product yourself, how can you convince someone else to believe it?" is the typical logic. This reasoning is anathema to the Japanese. Their own feelings are irrelevant or, better, taken for granted. If you are selling something, of course you like it. It goes without saying. Literally.

So, in Western parlance, the Japanese are most at ease when the product sells itself. In today's zero-defects climate, most Japanese companies can virtually guarantee perfect functioning. They don't view this as a competitive advantage over other Japanese competitors, although it may certainly be an advantage over others. What is more important is the "augmented" product, the brand image, the service and after-sales support, the negotiated price—and the implicit promise to the loyal customer (*okyakusama*) to match quickly any product improvement by competitors.

7

SETTING PRICES AND DOING ADVERTISING

The Japanese marketers overseas are generally competing on the basis of "value," offering quality products at very good prices. For example, Honda Accord has had several years of winning *Car and Driver*'s and *Consumer Reports*' best value awards. Toyota was rated highest in customer satisfaction among all companies in a cross-section of industries in Sweden. Reliability of Japanese consumer electronics products was so high that Western dealers, who used to rely on repairs and service for a large amount of their revenues, were compensated with fatter margins for the loss of business when they took on Japanese makes.

Although most Japanese companies think of the quality and function of their products first, "value" is created equally by a low price—which is why the Japanese companies abroad have tried very hard to refrain from price increases even in high yen times. This is basic marketing. Starting with the "value package" combining high product quality and low price, the Japanese then add value through their advertising and after-sales service with strong backing of distribution channels. Over time, the continuous product improvement and the gradual expansion into the upper end of the market enable the Japanese to offer the same value package at higher price points, still relying on advertising and service and adding image and status. If it sounds like a simple strategy, it is a simple strategy. But the point is how to execute it. That is the topic here.

JAPANESE PRICING

Pricing has always been a difficult topic for Western marketers. There are good reasons for this. First of all, even though pricing is part of the marketing mix, the marketing people do not completely control a product's price. Because prices minus costs of goods sold determine contribution margins and thus profits, accountants and top management usually monitor prices. Because of issues such as dumping and price discrimination, corporate legal counsel also watch a firm's price setting. Also, for consumers, low prices are a major competitive benefit; therefore, government policymakers watch price movements with interest.

Japanese companies are no different from Western corporations in these respects. If anything, the added complications of comparing prices in different countries make Japanese top management even more sensitive to price issues. Most consumers and companies alike know that prices of Japanese products in markets such as the United States tend to be lower than in Japan. For example, in 1995 a videocam model from Sony that in Japan cost 160,000 yen, or approximately $1,600, tax included, could be had in New York for about $950 plus 8.25 percent local sales tax. More than one top manager has defended the Japanese policy of not responding to exchange rate realignments by arguing that "otherwise Americans could not afford our products." Prices are clearly set on the basis not of costs but of sales volume, to keep market shares up.

Western marketers have reacted to the lack of marketing control by setting positioning list prices acceptable to all parties, and then making frequent short-term price changes. For example, temporary discounts and deals are common in packaged consumer goods, like soap, paper products, shampoo, and coffee. In addition, retailers and other middlemen often undercut manufacturers' list prices. Sometimes, as in autos, the basic model is a stripped-down version, with a myriad of optional features priced separately. And, sometimes, U.S. firms use multiple distribution channels, with different prices depending on the level of service and variety of models offered. In apparel, for example, you can buy a pair of Ralph Lauren shorts at the Ralph Lauren special boutique (high price), or in an off-price outlet or a wholesale club warehouse, with prices lower (but with higher risk of getting counterfeits).

The Japanese companies are not accustomed to dealing with prices in this manner. Fair trade is the norm, and resale price maintenance is standard in the home market. Further, the distribution system in Japan is often manufacturer-controlled, more rigid than in many Western markets. The Japanese corporations typically set their prices to provide middlemen with sufficient margins ("for the good of the trade"); they are not pleased by sudden price wars. Different brands, such as Sony, Panasonic, and Sharp, compete on the basis of product features and brand image, not price. Intra-brand price competition, where different distribution channels charge different prices for the same brand, is particularly disliked, and actively discouraged by MITI bureaucrats. The practice has been heresy for the Japanese manufacturers, which is one reason they have opposed the entry of large-scale discount chains such as Toys-R-Us, Wal-Mart, or Home Depot, where well-known brand names might be discounted. In the last couple of years this thinking has had to change as the price floor is gradually being eroded with the entry of new channels, but it still informs price policies of many companies.[103] More will be said on this in connection with distribution (see below).

NO TEMPORARY DISCOUNTS

Western marketers commonly distinguish between list (or recommended) price, and temporary price cuts. The list price is part of the positioning strategy: It sets the level at which consumers form their brand image and compare the brand to competitors. The temporary price cuts, used to move merchandise when sales are sluggish, are usually implemented as "specials," perhaps with coupons, in-store promotions, and rebates. The notion of "temporary" means that the cuts should not affect positioning. Intended to be short-lived, the price cuts have also tended to become fixtures.

The Japanese managers—and presumably many Western managers—abhor these "special deals" because they erode profit margins for both manufacturers and middlemen. They are not common in Japan, or even in Europe. Where lower price is a simple competitive benefit in the American economy, competition for the Japanese should not be about price but about product and service. They talk about competitive prices, but forego aggressive pricing as long as possible. Excessive price cutting is not a warrior's way to compete.

For many Western companies with experience competing against the Japanese, this attitude might seem hypocritical in extreme, in light of the U.S. dumping verdict against Japanese TV makers in the 1970s, the semiconductor price war before a trade agreement, and the fierce price cutting when copiers entered the Western markets.[104] How do such events square with the expressed Japanese sentiment?

The answer is quite simple. Japanese marketers and consumers view products in terms of specifications and brand image; therefore a new product or brand must have a relatively low entry price because no buyer would otherwise take a chance on the unknown brand. Given their traditions in the home market, this attitude is natural. The Japanese simply deal with customers who are much more risk averse than many in the West.

Thus, when a Japanese company enters a foreign market for the first time, the product usually enters with a very low price. In the past, this was at the lower end of the market. Today it is more likely to be at a higher price point—but relative to competition, lower prices are still common. This strategy differs from at least the American firms, and perhaps from some Europeans, who expect to exchange their success at home for a killing abroad. Firms from a variety of industries, such as McDonald's, IBM, Kodak, and General Electric, tend to flaunt their American market leadership as reason for premium prices abroad. European auto companies such as Volvo and BMW also use their foreign connection to extract consumer goodwill in the form of higher prices. So far, with less confidence in the status of their own country, the Japanese have largely avoided this strategy.

TARGET COSTING AND PRICING

As a Japanese company establishes its image abroad, you might expect the low-price entry tendency to weaken. But with a few possible exceptions, such as Sony, it is still unusual for a Japanese company to trade directly on its brand name to charge a price premium. And they still do not raise prices to higher levels because of large yen shifts, or to monopolistically gouge the customer later. Their objectives are much too long-term for such a profit-oriented tactic. Japanese prices abroad are generally set—and kept—at very competitive levels. One explanation for this price maintenance is their well-known preference for the long-term building of sales and market share over profits in the short run. Another is the consequent, anticipated reduction in cost due to the "experience curve" effect, that is, as sales and market share go up, the company's experience accumulates so that unit costs come down.[105] Also, even if existing competitors maintain higher prices, the actual or potential threat of other Japanese entrants puts a cap on price increases.

But the main factor at work is quite different. Unlike Western companies, Japanese companies do not set prices to provide a reasonable margin over costs in the long run. It's the other way around. Companies set prices so that the company can compete effectively in its markets—costs must come down to yield a profit at this price. While a Western pricing calculus treats production costs as given, Japan's unit production costs must accommodate a low enough price.

The Japanese call these practices target pricing, target costing, and value engineering. The company first analyzes the intended market to identify a target price, then sets the target costs so as to achieve a reasonable profit margin at that price. If the team cannot meet this cost target, it uses value engineering to pinpoint areas where costs can be reduced. The target costing and value engineering involve advanced analytical methods developed by Japanese engineers and described in recent publications.[106]

In selecting the target price, competitive pricing is the typical approach, in line with the positioning against competing brands discussed in Chapter 5. The actual target price chosen involves a tradeoff between product quality and functionality. Adding features increases functionality and justifies a higher target price, as do higher-quality materials and finer tolerances. The firm's feasible tradeoff possibilities among the target price, functionality, and quality is sometimes termed the "survival zone."[107] The choice of positioning in this zone involves a consensus among the product development team members drawn laterally from many functional areas, including design, production engineering, manufacturing, and marketing, within the firm.

This "constrained imagination" is typical of how the creative energies of the Japanese employees are challenged but at the same time disciplined. It represents brainstorming within well-contained borders. It is this type of mindset that might come up with a portable black-and-white television set, as Sony did in the 1960s, an electronic breadmaker that automatically starts making bread before dawn, as Matsushita did in the late 1980s, or the new "beercan" drum that Canon invented for its copiers in the 1980s. These are not the freewheeling inventions of an Apple computer, Edison's phonograph, or Carlson's Xerox, which depended on individual genius and daring. But once the basic notion has been born, and the imagination can focus on improving ease of use, extending the range of use, and using more efficient technology, the knowledge "spiraling" that results from the consensus process among the Japanese becomes a powerful method of creating new knowledge and new products.[108]

The derivation of the allowable cost target involves first subtracting a target profit margin from the target price. Target margins are typically based on forecast demand, planned product line, and long-term objectives. At Nissan, for example, the target margin is determined by ten-year profitability projections for existing and planned product mixes, given forecasted sales levels. When entering foreign markets with an existing product, the company chooses the price level typically based on competition in the market. But in these cases, the costs involved tend to be marginal costs rather than the average costs involved in the targeting approach; the company generally has more leeway in lowering prices when going abroad. Hence, many Japanese products are less expensive in the United States than in Japan, and not only because of swings in the exchange rates. Setting prices based on marginal costs, per standard micro-economic principles, becomes a powerful, competitive weapon when you factor in lifetime employment: Labor costs are essentially fixed and therefore do not add to marginal costs. The Japanese are accused of dumping in some overseas markets, but often unfairly so. Their low marginal costs can justify the low prices.

VALUE ENGINEERING

The first stage of value engineering involves comparing allowable costs to estimated costs, given existing operations. When the project team deems the difference too large and therefore unachievable, it reexamines the levels of functionality and quality, to drop allowable costs to realistic levels. Once the project team members agree on the new allowable costs, these costs become the target.

In the next step of value engineering, the team breaks down the allowable overall costs to isolate targets for subassemblies, components, and purchasing, based not just on current costs, but also on the team's experience and knowledge about new methods, materials, and competitors' practices. The company focuses in particular on those areas where allowable costs fall much below current costs, to identify possible cost reducing rationalizations and respecifications of the product overall. For example, in purchasing, Toyota offers high-cost suppliers special assistance (technical, financial) to introduce more modern equipment that will lead to reduced costs. The whole team evaluates the marketing risk of eliminating certain features, such as using plastic wheel covers instead of magnesium wheels. In contrast to many Western companies, where different functions intervene at different stages of the process, the whole product team is responsible throughout, so as not to jeopardize the integrity of the final product.

The mutual support system between supplier and principal has to be managed with care, especially in the startup stage when trust has not yet been firmly established. For example, when Honda first established its assembly plant for motorcycles (and later autos) in Marysville, Ohio, U.S. suppliers were recruited to raise the local-content percentage in the products. When the suppliers' standards were not up to the Japanese level, Honda offered the suppliers instructions in manufacturing techniques and quality control and even demanded new investment in machines. One supplier who had been asked to acquire a new stamping machine from a Japanese company claimed that the Japanese supplier had knowingly supplied faulty machine parts, aware that if the American company became a Honda supplier, the Japanese supplier would lose business. Honda denied the charges and they were never proven, but the case shows the difficulty when the close and tight-knit Japanese system was first transferred to the free market system of the West. Because of the Japanese successes with the system, however, most Western auto manufacturers have now shrunk their corps of suppliers, and attempt to work much more closely with the key remaining ones.

After each new improvement, the team computes the deviation of estimated costs from target costs to track the gradual improvement. When it reaches the allowable costs, it gives the go-ahead for production. If time is of the essence, as with me-too products, the team works around the clock to reach the cost target. When JVC developed the VHS format, for example, and RCA suggested a longer recording time at the same cost to make the tape competitive against Betamax, JVC's R&D department and product team managed some difficult technical development in less than four months. Value engineering is very much a manifestation of *kaizen*, the continuous improvement philosophy. Market information plays an important role in this process, since many of the cost-reducing design simplifications and reworkings involve consumer tradeoffs.[109]

The explanation for the target approach to pricing is, as always, the intense competition in the home market for the large exporting companies, less so for some not so competitive, domestically oriented industries, including chemicals, apparel, and services. The observed pricing pattern is actually what you would expect in freely competitive markets. Exhibit 7:1 features the typical diagram for price setting in perfect competition. With a horizontal demand curve, marginal revenue remains constant, and market forces set price. Firms are price takers, not price makers. To gain above normal profits the company must lower costs more than its competition. Hence, the Japanese company emphasizes making costs a function of the price and uses advertising and other promotional media to develop a superior image, sometimes the only differentiable advantage for a Japanese brand, in turn to generate a monopolistic "value added." But this value added translates into greater customer loyalty, not higher prices.

An experience curve effect also enters the price setting by the Japanese. As the sales of the product accumulate, the company learns new ways of manufacturing components, parts, simplified assembly, and so on. Furthermore, the company will pressure its independent suppliers to reduce costs and request their help to redesign parts and processes— the *kaizen* principle again.

Experience accumulates only with effort. Long and drawn-out discussions between marketing and manufacturing people about possibilities to focus cost cuts, redesign products, simplify assembly, and so on, grow

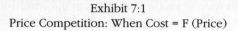

Exhibit 7:1
Price Competition: When Cost = F (Price)

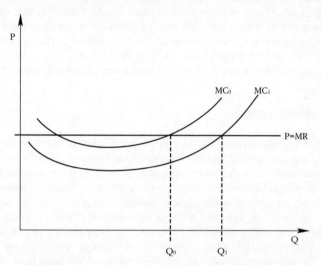

Lowering costs from MC_0 to MC_1 enables more profit and/or more revenues

into the tedious meetings in which so many Japanese company employees spend their time. Manufacturing might be lean—but even in efficient companies, "consensus" means face-to-face talking, as in Honda's free-for-all *wai-gaya* discussions mentioned in chapter 6. Cutting across functions, the "lateral" project team meetings serve as the cost reduction task force, where interactions are facilitated by the fact that, as we saw in chapter 1, many people in marketing have an engineering background. Many have already spent a considerable time in manufacturing in their career, rotated into different sections and functions and market areas as part of their lifetime employment pattern.

JAPANESE ADVERTISING

For marketers who constantly face competitors with almost identical products priced similarly and with comparable quality and functionality of features and performance, the idea of a "unique selling proposition" naturally seems perplexing. How could anything Japanese be truly unique? Since the target is often a competitive brand, to highlight the target position and specific product attributes in the advertising copy strikes the Japanese as crude, and in bad taste. Of course, comparative advertising makes sense when the nerve is strong enough, as in some Lexus newspaper ads that American dealers place in the United States, directly comparing prices with Mercedes. But you should expect Japanese managers to avoid direct attribute comparisons instinctively. The benchmarking and the reverse engineering have addressed the functional issues. There must be some value added, and advertising must help provide it.

IMAGE ADVERTISING

In the pricing discussion we saw how the Japanese must force costs down to survive in their intensely competitive home market. If the stress on value-added factors in advertising succeeds, then the company in fact creates an image that frees it from the price and cost squeeze. Exhibit 7:2 shows how creating a strong brand and a "feel good" quality actually allows the firm to operate with a downward sloping monopolistic demand curve, and gain more revenues through higher prices and/or greater quantities sold. This exercise in elementary price theory helps explain the Japanese drive for the "softer" value-added aspects of quality. Competitors can more easily benchmark and copy functional quality than advertising quality (although using the same ad agency is a step in that direction).

Thus, the Japanese advertisers are usually very intent on creating a strong brand image at home and abroad. Instead of selling or advertising features and specific test results, they try to create a "feeling," "dream," or "spirit" around their product (usually through a well-known spokesman, a unique cartoon figure, or a strong slogan) to distinguish themselves from the competition. This strategy gives products a more spiritual and symbolic meaning than in the West, with the TV commercials conveying the ultimate aspiration of many Japanese companies, namely the goal of "improving life."

Toyota's advertising in the United States demonstrates this thinking in action abroad. As president of Toyota North-America, Isao Makino spearheaded the rapid market penetration of the American market in the 1970s. His main contribution was changing the advertising: "Before, automobile advertising focused on the product, showing cars on the road and in staged settings. I suggested that the advertising focus on people, and what Toyota did for real people's lives." The result was the very successful "Oh, what a feeling" campaign. Such shifts may seem obvious winners in retrospect, but the execution by the agency has to be subtle. Some of Nissan's advertising, including the notorious Infiniti ads mentioned in

Exhibit 7:2
Functional Quality vs. "Feel Good" Quality
Atarimae Hinshitsu vs. *Miryoku Teki Hinshitsu*

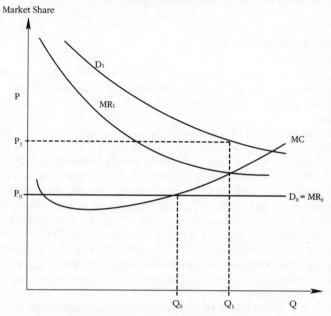

P_1-P_0 = Price Premium for "Feel Good" Quality
$P_1Q_1-P_0Q_0$ = Revenue increase due to "Feel Good" Quality
Q_1-Q_0 = Unit sales increase due to "Feel Good" Quality

chapter 6, has aspired to a similar focus away from the product and toward the loftier sentiments Nissan products inspire. While such advertising has been successful at home, in the United States the spots seem to have veered too far away from "real" people and situations. Nissan pulled its "Built for the human race" campaign after research showed negative audience reactions to the "pompous" message.[110]

When the revolutionary automatic SLR camera AE-1 was introduced in the mid-1970s, Tatehiro Tsuruta, head of Canon's U.S. operation, was responsible for the choice of John Newcombe, a tennis player, as the spokesman. "The first idea was to choose some popular football player, but as we did some screening of candidates and talked to agency representatives, it became clear that football players had mainly a strong local following, and were not liked everywhere, especially in a traditional opponent's home state. We decided to choose a star with no special affiliation to a particular city or state in the United States, and were lucky to find John Newcombe, the star tennis player. Tennis does not appeal to everyone, but for our target market, a bit upscale, the fit was good. John was Australian, and accepted everywhere."[111]

NONSENSE ADVERTISING

Companies have given the soft sell associated with image advertising a peculiarly nonsensical twist in Japan, where TV commercials sometimes leave the audience wondering which product or brand the ad was promoting.

Western observers of TV advertising in Japan are frequently struck by the soft-sell, fantasy-oriented approach used. An actor dances with the advertiser's product, a Pilot compass; a puppy walking through the rain creates the mood for a Suntory whisky; and a dentist extracts a patient's teeth to sell an insect spray from Kinchoru. An *Advertising Age* article, aptly headlined "Where mood speaks louder than words," traced the typical patterns in award-winning Japanese TV spots: The Japanese "avoid logic," an "articulate speaker is not to be trusted," and "effective communications are implicit, they are emotional rather than logical, they are intuitive." The oft-quoted slogan for Sapporo beer, third largest in Japan, is "A man drinks Sapporo without logic." Japanese advertising is thoroughly post-modern.[112]

The fact is that the lack of emphatic selling demonstrations, the limited exposure of unique features, the seemingly irrelevant usage situations, the preference for cartoon characters, and the popularity of persistently upbeat musical soundtracks all add up to a fantasy-filled, mood-creating, "unserious" audience experience in Japanese TV advertising.[113] Even though voice-overs and actors' dialogue sometimes clarify the message and articulate the sales pitch, the commercials remain subtle by comparison to the straightforward one-two-three benefit punch of most U.S. TV commercials.

Why the soft sell in Japan? How does soft sell at home affect Japanese practices abroad? First, there is unquestionably a cultural resistance among the Japanese against hard-sell advertising. When the seller views the buyer as "God," and the buyer takes high quality for granted, a Japanese seller who exhorts the virtues of a product too strenuously will be suspect (as the *Ad Age* feature noted). Furthermore, when an ad agency is able to serve several competing clients, as is common in Japan, copywriters may be reluctant to hit the superiority claims and unique selling propositions too hard, and direct comparisons, although increasingly accepted, are still rare, and are produced with some trepidation. When

Diet Pepsi took on compatriot Coca Cola Light (the name for Diet Coke in Japan) in a comparative newspaper ad in the early 1990s, the copy was typically polite and indirect: "To the person who likes calories: Warning. Diet Pepsi is not for you. We would recommend Coca Cola Light. The reason? Diet Pepsi has only 1/12 of Coca Cola Light's calories." At the bottom of the ad, below a photograph of a single Diet Pepsi can, visible is Pepsi's Japanese slogan rendered in English: "Pepsi loves you." Hardly U.S.-style comparative advertising.

At a deeper level, the Japanese hesitate to be transparently logical about the motivation behind a business transaction; they are uneasy with "instrumentality," the idea that advertising "stimulates" a certain behavior. The typical stimulus-response models that implicitly underlie much of mass communication efforts in the West are understood but foreign to Japanese thinking. They don't feel comfortable clearly stating their point of view, or elaborating on their brand's superiority over the competition's to influence people.

Where, then, do the Japanese consumers get real data about products and services? At the retail level. In Japan, the real learning about many products does not occur until the buyer is in the store. The store owners and salespeople, having spent most of their working lives in that particular industry and store, by and large understand how the products function, how they can be serviced and repaired, and why their particular customers might buy them (things rarely true of retailers in Western stores).

With more discount outlets and low-service convenience stores appearing, where in-store information is weak or lacking, preselling becomes important, and there is a shift toward more attribute-oriented advertising in some product categories. For detergent, paper products, shampoo, and over-the-counter drugs, specific selling propositions are now being seen more often. Combined with the traditional Japanese penchant for fastidious detailing of what exactly makes for the functioning of the product, and the Japanese lack of self-consciousness about bodily functions, the advertising is in some ways freer than elsewhere. For example, the way a baby's excretions penetrate and discolor a diaper, and how the "odor-eating" diaper counters the attack, is explicitly rendered through advanced animation techniques.

But for most of the consumer durable goods categories in which the Japanese are successful abroad, attribute advertising is still rare. Retail stores fulfill much of the informational function concerning product attributes, as well as the "high-touch" aspects of product examination, so that advertising can concentrate on building value-added image via soft-sell advertisements and commercials. Consumer choice is often a matter of selecting the brand image and the store with which one wants to be associated and feels most comfortable doing business. Without the support of the frontline retailers, the Japanese could not indulge in the preferred soft-sell advertising. As a result, when they go abroad, they painstakingly cultivate the members of their distribution channels, as we will see in the next chapter, far more than their Western counterparts.

REPOSITIONING A BRAND

As we have already mentioned, the value added by advertising helps to create some differentiation among otherwise very similar products that all have pretty much the required combination of features. In terms of the typical product-space diagram used to map out competitive positioning, the brands are clustered close together. The value added is a matter of the special image or identity of the brand, and does not translate into specific attributes in the space. By the same token that "Men drink Sapporo without logic," it is not useful to "explain" the choice of Sapporo with reference to its attributes. It's simply "that old feeling" again.

But there is also a place for advertising to create value added in the sense that image advertising can help reposition a brand. This has been used to some advantage by Western entrants to the Japanese market, especially by European producers. German engineering and quality, French style and high class, Italian designs and colors are elements of a foreign image that give imports from these countries a definite entry opportunity in Japan. The problem is, the products from these countries do not always live up to what Japanese customers expect in terms of functionality. The solution has been for the Japanese importers to do thorough delivery preparations, reworking some parts, and in more extreme cases reassemble the products. Although the companies at home have now improved, controls and finish of Western automobiles were routinely reworked on arrival in Japan. Benetton sweaters, French designer apparel, and German duvets sewn in Japan are consistently of higher quality than the corresponding products at home. Ironically, because of the reworking and the support from the Japanese importers' advertising, for the Japanese customers, European products still retain their cachet of extra-high quality.

Image-oriented value-added advertising campaigns are also used by some Western companies at home. Nike, for example, used the value-added thinking behind its successful use of advertising to regain the market leadership from Reebok. Just like the global industries where the Japanese are strong (autos, consumer electronics, cameras), the global sports shoe industry shows intense rivalry among several strong competitors. Technologically based development of new products ahead of customer preferences, tremendous proliferation of model variants destroying a company's own share leader, desperate attempts to copy new features quickly from competitors, targeting of very specific usage segments, and hands-on market research are all characteristics of the sport shoe market success formula. If you also emphasize creating brand and model images that enhance product usage over and above the immediate functional requirements, then you add value in your own right. Nike's strategy is very similar to the Japanese strategies described here.[114]

CORPORATE IDENTITY

Building a strong brand image is a key issue for Japanese marketers. They want to give the customer the assurance and status of a well-known brand name whenever possible. But brand image is only one aspect; they also want to support a favorable *company* image.

In Western markets, customers might recognize brand names, such as Tide, Minute Maid, and Frito-Lay, but they may not know or care which company stands behind the brands (Procter & Gamble, Coca Cola, and Pepsico, respectively). Corporate identity is not usually a very salient issue. In Japan, by contrast, corporate identity (CI) has enjoyed a boom since the late 1980s. Corporations have simplified their names, eliminating industry identifications and limiting their names to three initials if they could. For example, Computer Service Kaisha became CSK, Kao Soap became Kao, Toyo Kogyo became Mazda, the name already used overseas because of its founder Jujiro Matsuda's name, and NEC got rid of its traditional Nippon Electric Corporation. Customers have learned to connect a particular brand to a specific company. There is an additional level of customer security in knowing that the company behind a brand is large and well-recognized. Therefore, most Japanese communications conspicuously display the corporate name and logo: For example, the company name comes up at the end of many TV commercials ("Attack, from Kao") to reinforce both the brand name and the corporate image. Even Procter & Gamble now ends its Japanese commercials with the corporate initials "P&G."

Although companies like Intel ("Intel inside") or Disney do promote corporate image in Western markets, such practices tend to be less common during waves of mergers and acquisitions, when corporate identity becomes a moot issue. Then firms frequently focus on brand equity, exploiting well-known brand names like RCA in television sets (acquired by France's Thomson), Richardson-Vicks in health care products (bought by Procter & Gamble), and Magnavox (acquired by Dutch Philips), for example. Among the Japanese, Matsushita maintains Quasar, Denon uses

Macintosh, and Sanyo still features Fisher stereos.[115] But the Japanese instinct is to rename brands, a tendency held in check only by a greater desire not to attract too much negative publicity. Sony renamed Columbia records, first to CBS/Sony and then simply to Sony, and would like to do the same with the acquired Hollywood studios. Not simply arrogance and megalomania, the change reflects the desire to prove to the customer that the company stands behind its products, and to help employees unite and identify with a successful and growing business.

On the side of the employees, the corporate identity drive reflects the Japanese desire to "belong" to the corporation. The corporation's identity and the identity of the individual employee merge, a positive motivational effect. Overseas, Western individualism makes this morale booster less effective, although it clearly has been successful at the worker level in many countries. At management level, the employee effect can backfire, since some executives will feel uncomfortable with a corporate identity greater than their egos. The difficulties of Sony and Matsushita in managing their Hollywood acquisitions (Columbia Pictures and MCA, respectively) are perhaps extreme examples, but still illustrative of the basic conflict. Matsushita's sale of MCA to Seagram, and Sony's firing of Columbia's chief, Michael Schulhof, revealed deep rifts in management philosophies between the Hollywood executives and their Japanese principals. A similar problem surfaced at American Honda, when its U.S. sales executives were convicted of receiving illegal kickbacks from its dealers who needed extra allocations of Honda's successful models. While the Japanese companies might have been able to rely on organizational culture and individual discipline for controls at home, overseas business traditions are different, and more systematic control mechanisms are needed. And as the recent scandals at Daiwa bank in New York and at other banks in Japan demonstrate, when the stakes are high enough, even the Japanese can no longer resist indulging their egos.

AGENCY RELATIONS

When it comes to hiring an ad agency, the Japanese companies overseas turn to host country advertising agencies, not their Japanese agencies, whereas the American multinationals often rely on the local subsidiaries and affiliations of the American agencies. Thus, even though Western agencies have succeeded in going global in scope and clientele, most Japanese agencies do little work outside their home country and Southeast Asia. It's not simply that Americans do not want to adapt to local conditions. Of course, they probably feel more comfortable collaborating with the same agencies as at home, and the concurrent multinational expansion of the American and European agencies facilitates central control from U.S. or European headquarters. In addition, the local offices of the Western agencies often attract the best creative talents in the host country. So why don't the Japanese firms work with their own Japanese agencies overseas?

The surface answer is that the Japanese agencies don't have well-established offices overseas. There are a few joint ventures, such as the Dentsu with Young & Rubicam, and McCann-Erickson with Hakuhodo (now wholly owned by McCann). But why have the Japanese agencies not followed the West to establish branches and wholly owned subsidiaries overseas parallel to the Japanese business expansion? The deeper answer lies in the peculiar institutional and cultural conditions under which Japanese agencies operate at home.

First of all, advertising agencies in Japan are much more powerful business entities than U.S. and European agencies are in the West. The giant Dentsu agency controls many of the Japanese media vehicles available (including TV programs), and even produces some of the shows, and can accept work from clients who are also competitors by using different units within the organization to maintain confidentiality. Both of these factors work so as to give the agency more flexibility and greater power vis-à-vis the client base.[116]

A cultural reason for delegating most authority over advertising decisions to the agency is that media communication is, after all, a matter of blowing your own horn. The firm in a socially reticent society such as Japan naturally prefers an independent party to do the advertising, much like a go-between *nakodo* who arranges a marriage. Accordingly, the emphasis on image and brand name fits a preoccupation with form in social communication. As was mentioned above, the same impulse also guides the agency into developing copy with much less of a product-information or unique-selling-proposition approach. The agency uses more soft-sell approaches than can any hired agency in the West, because much of the product information is communicated through well-informed retailers in Japan and seasoned sales clerks. Western agencies lack this luxury.

Given the strength and idiosyncratic nature of the agency business in Japan, Japanese companies are accustomed to give a free hand to their advertising agencies. Apart from broad objectives and direction (such as Makino's admonition to "focus on the people" for Toyota), the execution is left in the hands of the agency people. But since the Japanese agencies' competency in the foreign media environment is limited, this agency is probably not one from Japan. The better adapted an agency is to the

Japanese home environment, the less suited it will be for operations abroad. The Japanese expansion abroad has been good for many Western agencies, especially welcome since the creative freedom offered by Japanese clients reluctant to impose their ideas on a foreign marketplace is greater than what the agencies are accustomed to.

8

THE
MIDDLEMEN
CUSTOMERS

Given the similarity of products, price, and advertising policies, the Japanese understandably emphasize competitive advantages in distribution channels. Distribution is one of the few areas left where true uniqueness can be created, and it is common in Japan for manufacturers to attempt to create their own distribution outlets. Leading market share holders in Japan are almost invariably companies whose superiority rests heavily on distribution coverage. Matsushita in consumer electronics, Kao in packaged goods, Shiseido in cosmetics, and Toyota in autos have long had competitive advantages in distribution, although as Japan's multitiered distribution system gets simplified and as large discounters appear, some of these advantages may be eroded. But although the traditional distribution system in Japan is presently undergoing a massive change, the basic philosophy that underlies Japanese marketers' approach to channel members is still intact.

Because channels in Japan have for so long been dominated by manufacturers, traditional retail stores might only offer one brand of a product. To do comparative shopping the consumer must search through several stores. The Japanese in the West attend closely to the role of distribution as a competitive advantage, partly as a consequence of the situation at home. In contrast, Western companies regularly deal with strong, independent channel members like superstores and vertically integrated retail chains, and therefore have less opportunity, skill, and imagination to nurture the kind of channel support that the Japanese have managed in the West.

CLOSE TO CUSTOMERS

In Western marketing thinking, distribution is important largely in terms of product or brand availability. Getting the product to the customer is the main job. This is clearly a real managerial headache in a country as large as the United States, where stores carry competitors' brands, where consumers view time as important, and where instant gratification is a learned reflex. A brand out of sight is out of mind, and the firm is out of business. If they can't see the brand they intended to buy, customers will switch to another brand. Of course, with the emergence of the Internet as a new marketing medium, some of these conditions can be expected to change.

In contrast, distribution in the geographically much smaller Japan is important because it is the arena where the customers get information, where they learn about products, and where the "moments of truth" come, to use Jan Carlzon's phrase about personal service.[117] "Thank you for coming to our store," is a typical Japanese greeting, signifying the importance of the visit. The thanks in a Western store come only at the final purchase, if even then, and many store owners in the West still find browsers a nuisance, sneering at them because they might leave without buying. Small wonder if catalog buying and Internet shopping are on the upswing.

The distinction might seem minute, but informs subsequent management behaviors. In recent years, American managers have often been accused of being out of touch with their customers and their middlemen. The Japanese (and some exceptional Western managers like Sam Walton) have then often been put forward as the prototypes for the new types of managers, who stay close to the customers. Stories about Japanese executives visiting each American dealership at least once a year are contrasted with Detroit's lack of involvement—clearly a somewhat unfair comparison, considering the number of dealers involved in each case, and the American tradition of arm's-length relationships.[118]

CHANNEL CUSTOMERS

The tight-knit distribution system in Japan goes with Japanese managers overseas. The Japanese tend to view their independent channel members as part of the "family." Eiji Toyoda said, "First come our customers, then our dealers, then our employees."[119] Although not unknown in the West, such familial sentiment is the exception. One of the major topics in marketing channel analysis is the resolution of conflict. *For the Japanese, such conflict is a result of bad management.* It should not occur. As we will see, however, as distribution in Japan opens up to cheaper imported products, even Japanese companies will resort to legal tactics, if necessary, to control wholesalers and retailers.

Most Japanese firms successful in foreign markets function basically as the channel "captains" at home and abroad. That is, they exercise power over the other members of the channel. This dominance is acceptable to foreign distributors because the Japanese are often share leaders in their selected market segments and because the Japanese companies offer strong support in the channels. Dominance is feasible for the Japanese because of skills developed at home, where manufacturers often control the whole vertical chain down to the ultimate consumer. It is their preference, since the Japanese managers can then fully act out that paternal instinct which seems to come naturally to their business relationships. It's "all in the family."

The typical Western pattern of channel organization focuses on efficiencies. As shown in Exhibit 8:1, the middlemen position themselves to minimize costs for the channel transactions.

Exhibit 8:1
Keeping Close to the Customer: Western Distribution

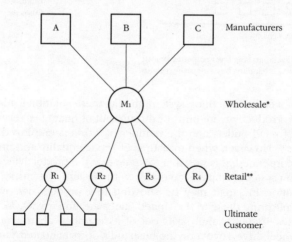

*Few, handling many competing brands.
**Few large chains, handling all competing brands.

A central clearing point for the collection, rearrangement, and dispersion of merchandise has long been a hallmark of American marketing, codified in particular by Wroe Alderson.[120] The traditional Japanese way without a central clearing point involves much more control by manufacturers (see Exhibit 8:2).

Exhibit 8:2
Keeping Close to the Customer: Japanese Distribution

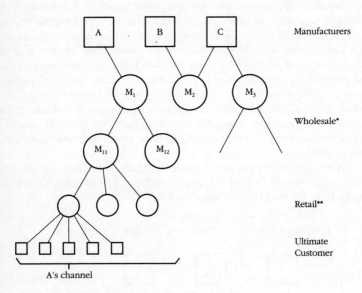

*Many, each handling few competing brands.
**Many, each handling few competing brands.

For the overall distribution system, the Japanese solution leads to lower efficiency. Productivity in terms of throughput of quantities relative to the number of retail outlets and the number of workers employed is generally lower.[121] However, when measures of service quality and price stability are incorporated, it is possible to argue that the productivity of Japan's distribution system compares favorably with Western systems.[122]

Distribution in Japan may be showing low productivity overall, but changes mirroring those in the United States are under way. As the modern Japanese big-city family gets out of its cramped apartment and into its four-wheel drive Toyota on the husband's now-mandated Saturday off, with the kids tucked into the backseat, they are likely to head for the shopping malls dotting the landscape outside town. There they can shop in Daiei, Uno, or Ito-Yokado superstores that are indistinguishable from many Western superstores, while the children roam through the Toys-R-Us store next door. If one wonders where all the purchases are stored, the same question can be raised in many Western homes as well. As always, when distribution becomes more efficient, it is often because storage and transportation functions are shifted to consumers.

MARKET LINKS

The advantage is, of course, that the Japanese manufacturer has a direct link to the market. The Japanese marketer easily stays close to the ultimate consumer, as shown in Exhibit 8:3. Channel members directly depend on one manufacturer who may help with trade and other financing. In return, the dealer may sell only one manufacturer's brand. This manufacturer can easily divert shipments away from a recalcitrant retailer. Retailers have few if any options to develop alternate supplies, or to work away from their stores. They see their jobs as lifetime occupations, and learn about the products and the customers. The manufacturer can invest in training service personnel and in demonstrating new gear. Not surprisingly, the manufacturer can easily get the cooperation of retailers to report customer sentiments on a regular basis. At least in Japan, travel distances are small, and visiting and sharing experiences with the dealers becomes a natural. *In Japan, staying close to the customer usually means visiting one's dealers.*

Exhibit 8:3
Close to Customers

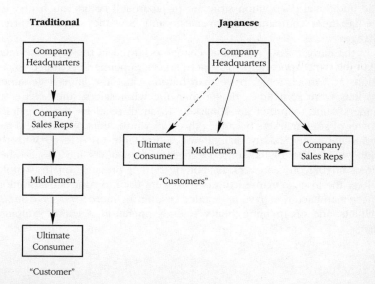

Traditional

Company Headquarters

Company Sales Reps

Middlemen

Ultimate Consumer

"Customer"

Japanese

Company Headquarters

Ultimate Consumer / Middlemen ◄──► Company Sales Reps

"Customers"

Control over distribution is often cited as a reason for the dominance of some Japanese manufacturers in their home market. Shiseido in cosmetics, Kao in packaged household goods, and Matsushita in electronics are typical examples, as are Kirin in beer and Coca Cola in soft drinks. Shiseido supports retailers with deep services, including inventory control, shelf stocking, sales training, and store demonstrations. Kao has assumed the wholesaling function for its products (detergents, shampoos, soaps, diapers, and related products), and supplies retailers from its distributors located throughout Japan. Matsushita's brands (National, Technics, Panasonic) and products are sufficiently many to support retailers selling Matsushita products only, and even though the Matsushita stores consolidate during the ongoing structural changes, National's advantage in the Japanese market rests on good, reliable products—and wide distribution. Kirin's market leadership and its wide distribution, including a large number of vending machines, induced Budweiser to shift its distribution partner from Suntory to Kirin.[123] The Coca Cola story is similar. Coca Cola, by adding products such as isotonic drinks and coffee to its product line could economically set up its own vending machines in the bigger cities and railroad stations throughout Japan, creating a dominant presence for the brand.

STRUCTURAL CHANGES

The traditional distribution structure in Japan still colors much of what the Japanese companies do overseas, and how they react to current changes.

In the early 1960s, a dramatic change occurred in the Japanese retail channels—the appearance of supermarkets. Supermarkets aimed to sell goods at a much lower price than before. Since the large-scale supermarkets were sometimes bigger than the wholesalers, and since consumers came to prefer supermarkets to small retailers, the bargaining power of supermarkets became a threat to wholesalers. Wholesalers had to reduce prices, barely maintaining a profitable price level. With the high yen in the 1990s, some of these supermarkets have established direct buying offices overseas, putting further pressure on the wholesalers, and also on manufacturers who were used to control distribution. These manufacturers have responded by offering more services to supermarkets, and streamlining their wholesale operation. A good example is Kao.

THE KAO HANSHA

Kao first established an exclusive marketing subsidiary (a Hansha) in the Kyushu area in Southern Japan. The subsidiary handled all the Kao products as a distributor to smaller wholesalers and larger retailers in southern Japan. When the new distribution system succeeded, Kao expanded the wholesale subsidiary concept all over Japan. By 1970, the number of marketing subsidiaries had risen to 128, later consolidated into 22 large units. With its strong marketing and distribution division, Kao was able to maintain projected price levels despite the power of supermarkets.

Internalizing the distribution with the Kao Hansha served to stabilize the Kao product flow and build an entry barrier against competitors such as Kanebo, Lion, and P&G Japan, which relied on independent distribution channels. It gave Kao the ability to bypass two layers of sales agents. Furthermore, the Kao Hansha allowed Kao to specialize and divide the company according to manufacturing and marketing functions. Manufacturing had to support the Hansha. which required high-speed product introduction and product proliferation. The Hansha also helped Kao sharpen its abilities in R&D, distribution operations, and market information feedback.[124]

After 1990 as the integrated vertical distribution system came under pressure from discount outlets featuring cheaper imports, Kao has responded by consolidating warehouses and wholesalers, offering more co-op advertising support to independent channel members, and increasing missionary salespeople to offer shelving, displays, and in-store advertising support. In addition, the company has pruned its various product lines (shampoos, detergent, toothpaste, paper products), offering fewer variants, concentrating on the top two brands in each line, and eliminated some lines (such as a new line of cosmetics, Sofina). The actions seem to have been successful, as similar efforts by Shiseido and Matsushita have been, at least for the time being, and if the yen stays over one hundred to the dollar, one would expect the channels to remain competitive.

CONSUMER CLUBS

In addition to extensive coverage of retail outlets (Matsushita has more than three times the retail outlets of Sony, for example), the traditional channel captains from manufacturing have also gone to great lengths to engender loyalty among customers, middlemen as well as ultimate consumers. Shiseido has long run a Shiseido Club, for example, where its loyal customers get news of new products, invitations to special events featuring fashion and cosmetics, discount coupons for new introductions, a chance to participate in product testing, and free samples. Consumers are eligible to join even without purchase of a Shiseido product, but pay a small fee to become a member. The fee is not intended simply to cover costs, but rather serves to raise the commitment level among members.

Although the club concept has spread to the cosmetics industry in the West, in Japan it has long been common in other product categories as well, especially in target markets with young people. Department stores create clubs that tie into the now common store cards, electronics manufacturers offer discounts to loyal club members, and record stores give discounts to club members.

Clubs are not necessarily limited to the immediate promotion of products and services either. In addition to frequent flier programs, travel agents and airlines organize travel clubs. Camera manufacturers create photography clubs and run contests, and leisure wear makers sponsor exercise clubs. Yamaha, the musical instrument company, has started its own music school and sponsors music education clubs. Even a foreign company such as Procter & Gamble Japan has developed its own Pampers club. The clubs demonstrate how the products and services enhance a person's life, like the many clubs (languages, hiking, motor) that the Japanese join at an early school age. Japanese consumers understand the benefits well, especially in terms of reducing the perceived risk of consumer choice, and the Japanese are well-adapted to the limits on individual preferences and behavior that membership entails.[125]

These intimate manufacturer ties with middlemen and consumers naturally become barriers to entry for outsiders. A big problem when penetrating the Japanese distribution system is that these links multiply into a tightly interwoven network between manufacturers, wholesalers, retailers, and consumers, links that are difficult to disentangle also for Japanese middlemen, should they wish to. Since the network leads to inflexibilities that make it difficult to shift to new and more efficient channel alternatives, these barriers are eroding as the Japanese distribution system gradually opens up.

The preoccupation of the manufacturers with existing middlemen and consumers can lead to a narrow focus on a particular market and limiting expansion elsewhere. The entry barriers of loyal customers become immobile "location-specific" advantages, which the company has learned to exploit. In markets where the barriers are not so high or not yet created, competition shifts ground, and the company might lack capability to perform. Both Shiseido and Kao have encountered problems in their expansion abroad, partly because they cannot easily replicate their domestic strength in distribution in foreign markets. Approaching foreign markets, the companies decided that creating similar channels abroad would be too expensive and risky. Instead they were forced to devise new channel configurations with which they have little experience. As mentioned before, Shiseido spent over a decade selling through drugstores when entering the U.S. market, not realizing that the key channel was upscale department stores. Kao could not use power with the independent retail chains in the United States since their leading brands in Japan were unknown there, and decided to buy Jergens, a Cincinnati company, to gain at least some distribution access.

KEIRETSU BREAKUPS?

As you know by now, the tightly integrated distribution channels, sometimes called vertical *keiretsus,* have recently come under pressure from structural changes in Japanese retailing. The structural impediments initiative (SII), a 1988 trade agreement between the U.S. and Japanese governments, in which the Japanese agreed to open up their distribution system, helped foreign retailers such as Toys-R-Us enter Japan. The strong yen and the consequent parallel trade in cheaper imports, as well as the recession-induced search by Japanese consumers for low prices, are also factors contributing to this change. The "close to the middleman" and "close to the customer" ways in Shiseido, Kao, and Matsushita are based on labor-intensive person-to-person interactions, and thus costly. If the brands are discounted, gross margins shrink and profits evaporate, and manufacturers are even using legal tactics, unusual for Japan, to make sure retailers toe the line. A Shiseido example is illustrative.

In the early 1990s a battle took place between the Shiseido chain and a small cosmetics shop, called Fujiki Honten, in Tokyo's traditional Asakusa district.[126] In May 1990, Shiseido abruptly canceled its twenty-eight-year-old agreement with the small company. The proprietor of the store, Ken Fujisawa, had been selling Shiseido products during most of that period at a 20 percent discount, mostly through catalogs sent to the general affairs departments of large companies and circulated among women in the offices.

Selling at a discount was technically against the agreement, but enforcement of the rule would run counter to the anti-monopoly law. Shiseido therefore based its cancellation on the requirement that Shiseido's products be sold face to face. Since Fujisawa had sold through catalogs for more than two decades, and since some of Shiseido's own subsidiaries were selling over the phone, Shiseido was not on very solid ground.

The problem for Shiseido was that Fujisawa's store was no longer small. With Shiseido having 1.2 billion yen in annual sales nationwide, a large portion of its dominant brands were sold at discount prices, creating difficulties for Shiseido's loyal stores. But Fujisawa did not play dead. He filed a complaint with the Fair Trade Commission for violation of the anti-monopoly act. After a year of inaction, the FTC rejected the complaint, not surprising considering that Shiseido's chairman sits on the external review board of the commission. Fujisawa then turned to the Tokyo District Court and won a ruling in his favor. On September 27, 1993, Shiseido was ordered to resume shipping products to Fujiki Honten. Shiseido appealed the verdict, not resuming shipments "no matter what," but lost the appeal. Such legal moves are largely a delaying tactic—the tightly connected vertical distribution chains are gradually opening up, even in Japan.

INFORMATION SYSTEMS

Partly because of the price competition at retail levels, another structural change is under way in the Japanese distribution system: an explosion in the use of information technology to increase efficiency. Although the use of computer hardware and software in offices and homes still lags behind the United States and Europe, Japanese wholesalers and retailers have turned to the new information technology avidly. Point-of-sale (POS) terminals (not to be confused with POS, the Panasonic Ordering System created by the National Bicycle Manufacturing Company mentioned in chapter 3) have proliferated in stores, catalog shopping is growing rapidly, and computer-based networks linking manufacturers, wholesalers, and retailers have expanded to include delivery companies, suppliers, and specialist service providers. Ito-Yokado, the Japanese supermarket parent of 7-Eleven, has developed the most advanced applications.[127]

In Japan, every time a customer buys an item of merchandise at a 7-Eleven store, the sales clerk enters that customer's sex and apparent age, data that the computer links to the item-specific information captured by the bar code. This linkage enables detailed analysis of sales by customer attributes, and allows the store manager to determine who buys what and when. Not only does the store get useful ordering information, the display of the merchandise can be varied throughout the day to appeal to different segments. The early morning commuter, the ten o'clock shopping housewife, the midday crowd, the afternoon end-of-classes youngsters, and the late evening stragglers, all can be targeted by shifting up front features in stores that may stay open all night.

Exhibit 8:4 shows the extensive data available from one 7-Eleven store's POS system. It shows the extent of the networking involved, with ties to wholesalers and manufacturers, and with partners in Japan and the United States. The information is displayed on the graphic ordering terminal in a store, and the system helps track and validate the forecasts of turnover made when ordering various items. Ito-Yokado is adapting the system for use in its other stores as well, including those in the United States, with the aim of making it possible for frontline sales clerks to use expert systems to order goods on-line.

The impact of POS is felt by manufacturers across the board. It is no longer sufficient to maintain strong relationships and expect retailers to take the long view. Retailers can tell immediately when a product is not selling, and this is magnified nationwide in the case of the chain stores. Nonperforming items are being cut, and availability on the shelf is jeopardized unless a new product shows definite promise. Just as in the United States, the precision and timeliness of point-of-sale information has shifted the balance of power from manufacturers to retailers and wholesalers with market access.

Kao's Hansha have long been leaders in POS systems. To support its integrated system, Kao has used its Hansha to lead the change toward new information systems in retailing. Kao has helped to install computerized POS systems that directly connect the retailers to Kao's Hansha. The company's field representatives instruct the stores in automated scanner operation, daily reporting of sales, profitability on a per-brand basis, and how to optimize inventory. These augmenting services help Kao to retain control of its channels, maintain close links with retailers, and track sales daily in each local market.[128]

CLOSE TO FOREIGN MIDDLEMEN

Even if manufacturer-controlled distribution channels seem to obsolesce in Japan, the Japanese manufacturers, by transferring their customary way of business to the West, are transforming the vertical relationships in distribution channels, especially in the United States. In a larger version of MBWA (management by walking around), the Japanese manage channels by flying around.

MANAGEMENT BY FLYING AROUND

Patiently and persistently building personal relationships with their distributors and dealers, the Japanese have in fact created lifelong ties. By offering thorough training programs for dealer employees, they have improved their distributors' capability to provide customer service. Recognizing that zero-defect products eliminate profitable after-sales service work for dealers, they have offered extra compensation for lost opportunity.

Some of the moves are less revolutionary, but no less important. By giving steep dealer discounts, they have built goodwill toward sales of their products over competition. By aiming for high sales volumes, the Japanese maintained high turnover in the stores. Distributors and retailers all over the world who have dealt in Japanese products during the last two decades have done well.[129] As mentioned earlier, the high quality and reliability of Japanese products have actually led to dealers receiving compensation for the lack of previously lucrative repair business. Abuses have occurred, as in the case of Honda in the United States, where dealers who wanted increased allocations of popular models bribed some of Honda's American managers. After all, the early Civics, for example, sold well above list price. Apparently some of the economic surplus found its way into the pockets of American Honda's executives rather than the company, but for many Japanese managers and dealers some kind of rebate arrangement is not an unusual way of doing business. Being close to middlemen and customers involves not only business talk, but often perks, such as gifts for the spouse, free trips, and golf.[130]

The personal visits, patterned after their Japanese practice where they are so much easier to do, are really the key. They are of course team builders and motivators. "In Japan we call them whisky management tools," says Kiyonori Sakakibara, a management professor from Tokyo. But the visits are also occasions for hardheaded problem solving. "I find that out of ten complaints, five can be settled directly, three are based on misunderstandings, and only two remain for any lengthy discussions," claims Isao Makino, head of Toyota North America in the 1980s.

And the visits help in keeping track of sales and customer trends. "On my trips to the U.S., I usually try to observe and talk to some customers when I visit the stores," says Matsushita's Sakon Nagasaki, an executive at corporate headquarters back in Osaka. "There is no substitute for the real feel of customers in a store."[131]

The tight relationships with channel members naturally lead to better customer service. The more the middlemen knows and care about the product, the greater their efforts and the better their performance. There is also a payoff in the speed and completeness with which they provide access to market information. Middlemen to whom management has listened will more likely send monthly sales reports and pass along customer and competitive information. With the company-provided training, they are more likely to learn what information to observe and record.

Since success makes them stay, the middlemen whom the Japanese man-ufacturers visit will likely have more experience in and knowledge of the marketplace.

The manufacturers are not alone in introducing Japanese-style changes in the American distribution system. When Ito-Yokado first acquired the 7-Eleven license for Japan, the company adopted much of the American-based chain's franchised operations. One major change that proved cru-cial was made, however. Rather than insisting that all store franchises operate strictly by the manual, Ito-Yokado permitted local managers to innovate, adding products, changing store layout, and providing local ser-vices. The stores, not very welcome by competing Japanese retailers, had to be "good citizens," and local initiatives were encouraged and sup-ported by roving Ito-Yokado field supervisors. This approach helped motivate the store managers, and proved resilient when competing con-venience stores entered the market.[132]

By contrast, the American insistence on following the 7-Eleven "book," which simplified controls, mandated less training, and required only intermittent personal contact, allowed once-successful 7-Elevens to stag-nate. Absent management proved disastrous as new products took too long to introduce, shifting traffic and shopping patterns that jeopardized a location were not taken into account, and layout innovations by new competitors were not matched. Facing bankruptcy, the 7-Eleven parent company was sold to Ito-Yokado. The subsequent resurgence in 7-Eleven performance in the United States was mainly due to the management practices and in-store information systems transferred from the new Japanese parent.

CREATING CHANNELS

How are new Japanese channels established in a new foreign market? Again, the answer is: by hands-on research of existing practices and by trial and error. Sony bungled its first attempt to enter the U.S. market, by partnering with a distributor who did not have the resources or will to market the company's new transistorized radio. When Shiseido first entered the U.S. market, the company dealt directly with the drugstore chains, who extracted high dealer margin and gave lackluster support. By redirecting the effort via the large department stores, Shiseido belatedly managed to crack the market. Bell & Howell did not support Canon cam-eras in the 1950s, and a complete shift into its own distribution via spe-cialty retailers started Canon's move into the leading share position. And, of course, many companies have preferred to take a less direct route, using licensing, and original equipment manufacturing (OEM) arrange-

Exhibit 8:4
Information Flow and Physical Distribution Flow

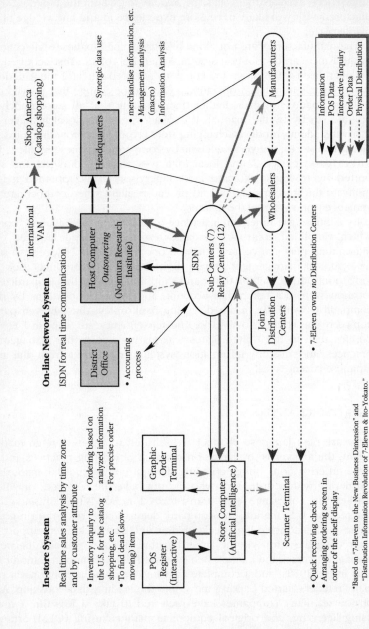

In-store System

Real time sales analysis by time zone and by customer attribute

- Inventory inquiry to the U.S. for the catalog shopping, etc.
- To find dead (slow-moving) item

- Ordering based on analyzed information
- For precise order

On-line Network System

ISDN for real time communication

Shop America (Catalog shopping)

International VAN

Host Computer *Outsourcing* (Nomura Research Institute)

Headquarters

- merchandise information, etc.
- Management analysis (macro)
- Information Analysis
- Synergic data use

District Office

- Accounting process

ISDN
Sub-Centers (7)
Relay Centers (12)

Manufacturers

Wholesalers

Joint Distribution Centers

- 7-Eleven owns *no* Distribution Centers

Graphic Order Terminal

Store Computer (Artificial Intelligence)

POS Register (Interactive)

Scanner Terminal

- Quick receiving check
- Arranging ordering screen in order of the shelf display

Information
POS Data
Interactive Inquiry
Order Data
Physical Distribution

*Based on "7-Eleven to the New Business Dimension" and "Distribution Information Revolution of 7-Eleven & Ito-Yokato."

ments. Ricoh's copiers were long sold under Savin's name, Canon still makes some of the Xerox copiers, and Mitsubishi cars are still distributed by Chrysler in the United States (although a dual system is now under development).

In autos, the record is very good. Nissan and Toyota did well from the beginning by tying up with existing dealers for American and European cars when their market shares were still relatively low—a deviation from Japan, where large sales make dual distributorships unnecessary. Honda's motorcycles were sold from the beginning through newly created dealerships, an expensive and slow process that has paid off handsomely (and that generated experience put to good use when the new Acura dealerships were established in the 1980s).[133]

The initial choice of distribution channels is really a matter of the usual drawn-out process of firsthand observation and keen judgment. Canon's search for a new channel arrangement after the breakaway from Bell & Howell, described in chapter 3, illustrates the typical approach. And once the channel is configured and the distributors and dealers selected, the Japanese provide a lot of technical support, product information, and sales training. In autos especially, where after-sales service is crucial for customer satisfaction, the Japanese dealers have been given unprecedented levels of support, and in the United States the Japanese have created a whole new level of quality service. In consumer electronics and cameras, the effort has mainly been directed at providing product information and reliable deliveries. Because of the zero-defect mentality, Japanese products have reached levels of reliability and workmanship where after-sales repairs, traditionally a good source of income for a dealer, have been significantly reduced. In fact, in the West it has been necessary for some Japanese manufacturers to offer higher dealer margins, rebates, and discounts precisely because the dealer cannot count on profitable after-sales service work. The middleman is a customer too.

9
PUTTING IT
ALL TOGETHER

At the end of the day, the proof of the pudding is in the eating. Is the Japanese emphasis on intuition and knowledge of the context in predicting customers, on the incremental strategies and continuous churning, and on the redefinition of the role of buyers and sellers, superior to the traditional Western reliance on more scientific methods? We think they are, and they have proven to be superior in markets where customer knowledge is high and the products are complex. But we also think that the Japanese approach dominates more distanced and less intensive scientific approaches in most contexts, and that if the Japanese thinking moves into other markets—high tech, consumer packaged goods—the Japanese will prove dominant again. This is why the new books, such as *Inside the Tornado* and *The Discipline of Market Leaders*, argue for approaches that are similar to the Japanese style described here.

But, as with everything, there is a downside. We will start this final chapter by talking about the myopia of the Japanese, and how it can lead to trouble. Then the chapter will summarize the major points of the Japanese approach, and will finish with some pointers for all marketers.

Marketing Myopia

Simply stated, the actual and potential drawbacks of the Japanese practices—and their thinking—fall under the category of shortsightedness, of tunnel vision. The marketing myopia that Levitt warned about back in 1960 is not hard to spot in many Japanese marketing practices.[134] The incrementalism, the targeting of existing brands, the competitive churning, the target pricing, the intricate bonding with existing customers and middlemen—all point to the same preoccupation with immediate action and reaction. Against this stands some exceptions—the value added from image advertising, the attempt to imagine the users' "mindset" for new product extensions, new technology—but when compared to Western marketers, the balance is clearly on the side of speed and flexibility in execution, not on innovative thinking about strategy. But how can firms with a long-term view be shortsighted? Is it not the Western firms that suffer from myopia?

THE LONG VIEW

The Japanese companies' traditional long-term perspective is well-known. Unlike Western firms that must satisfy individual shareholders' short-term expectations, the interlocking ownerships between *keiretsu* firms provided patient capital. Low labor mobility, lifetime employment, culture, religion, and even repentance over World War II enhanced this long-term posture.[135] The weakening of the financial markets, the recession, and the high yen rate in the early 1990s have combined to lessen these factors, but the long-term view is still evident in many companies' reluctance to lay off people and discard suppliers. And as the yen rate again rises above one hundred to the U.S. dollar, they return to the old ways.

The Japanese companies' preoccupation with the quality of their products and detailed technical specifications has also become well-known in the West. Their meticulous attention to detail, their focus on precise specifications, their desire to reach perfection in all aspects of their operations—as in the company wide quality control (CWQC) movement—are aspects of their organizations that have received a great deal of Western coverage.[136]

The Western observer spies the paradox: On the one hand, the Japanese are pedantics of the long view, the broad perspective, the creation of the future. Simultaneously, they are fanatics of detail, the here-and-now, the point of sale, the effervescent present. Yin and yang?

THE FUTURE IS NOW

Yes, yin and yang. The explanation is quite simple, if you reflect upon the meaning of a long-term view. What does the phrase connote to you? To most Westerners it means setting precise, measurable objectives further into the future. Instead of watching weekly share price fluctuations, quarterly sales reports, or thirteen-week ad campaigns, long-view managers fix their eyes firmly on three-year sales targets and five-year expansion roll-outs into some emerging markets. Small variations of execution toward these longer-term goals should not cause deviation from the course.

The Japanese long-term thinking is far more diffuse and imprecise, an allegiance to the longevity of the company and its people, rather than a well-articulated objective. It is that vague "vision" which so many Japanese company spokesmen spout, but is hard for Westerners to take seriously. It is so patently *tatemae*, the public face, the politically correct way of talking, not *honne*, the real intent, or true feeling. On an individual basis, few Japanese take it seriously either, but it has a social significance that makes it important. As with the notion that "the customer is God," for the Japanese the desired public image affects behavior much more than private convictions and doubts.[137]

The function of the long-term goal in the Western setting is to make sure that actions are geared to achieving the goal. "Means/end" chains linking alternative actions to the ultimate objective are spelled out, directions are given, and so on. By contrast, the vision is spelled out in the Japanese company so that the employees become invigorated, can stop worrying about it, and can get on with the business at hand.

Exhibit 9:1 attempts to clarify these differences using the image of climbing a mountain to represent the long-term objective.[138] The Westerner always keeps the objective in firm view, sees the path to the top, and focuses all efforts on reaching the top. The Japanese counterpart looks to the path itself, assumes that there is a peak to reach, and is not stopped by a clouded objective. Both behaviors, of course, are organically linked with the "scientific" (Western) versus "incrementalist" (Eastern) approaches discussed in earlier chapters.

Who is more long-term oriented? We know the answer is the Japanese. How can that be? The answer is that looking five years rather than one year into the future does not make for a long-term orientation. The only thing—repeat, the only thing—that matters is what one does (and doesn't do) today.

Exhibit 9:1

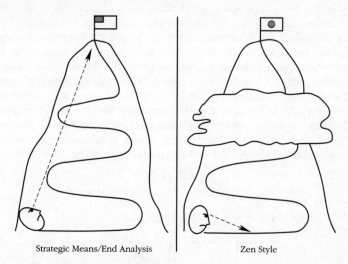

Strategic Means/End Analysis   Zen Style

THE ZEN OF REACHING THE GOAL

Keeping eyes on the peak, the Western climber easily stumbles on the path, is tripped up by small rocks. The Westerner ignores the environs and fellow climbers, takes shortcuts, tires of the distance, revels mildly in discernible progress, and rejoices at finally reaching the top, and only then. Pretty miserable.

In contrast the Japanese easily deals with obstacles in the path, deviating when necessary, returning farther up the slope. The Japanese will "hurry slowly," taking one step at a time, avoiding "smart" but potentially hazardous shortcuts. Celebration does not hinge on reaching the top. The climb itself is the raison d'être—from the top you see only higher mountains to climb.

Can you place the two climbers in the context of their respective companies? The Western climber is individualistic, takes greater risks, and likely reaches the top first. The Japanese climber plods steadily, and will not lose the way. The first climber is fired up, could get impatient, and could burn out. The second climber is patient, shows greater stamina, is a marathoner.

The long-term view of the Japanese managers affects how they approach their everyday tasks. They pay attention. They do things well. They nurture their fellow workers. They reap what they sow.

Such an approach lends itself to quality improvement. Exhibit 9:2

shows the basic picture. The Japanese soak up details that Westerners miss. The "big picture" orientation of the Westerner filters out minor deviations. In the West improvised quick fixes, such as replacing leather with vinyl trim on dashboards, are improvised on the spot by impatient cost cutters, assuming that "the customer won't notice it." Japanese managers and customers alike do notice it. Japanese customers hesitate to buy apparel where the label is not sewn on perfectly aligned. It is a sign of low quality. Since competitors' products with high quality and perfect merchandise are available, why take a chance? Distributors know this, and return goods to the manufacturers for minor blemishes. When Bosch, the German electric machinery manufacturer and supplier to Mercedes and BMW, first started exporting to Japan, products were returned because the Bosch name plate was not perfectly horizontal.

Exhibit 9:2
The Quality Problem: A Matter of Discrimination

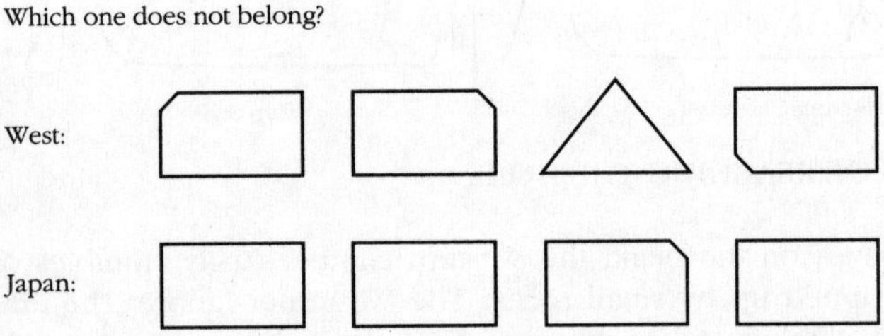

Which one does not belong?

West:

Japan:

Although the recession and low prices on imports have induced some Japanese consumers to be less picky, they still pay attention to detail, calculating exactly how much of a sacrifice they make. With the high yen making Western products very cheap, it is not surprising if American goods are making inroads in Japan—what is perhaps more impressive is the fact that some Western firms have succeeded in approaching the Japanese quality standards.[139]

MYOPIA REVISITED

The weakness of myopia in business was first brought out in Levitt's classic *Harvard Business Review* article, "Marketing Myopia."[140] Levitt showed how the American railroad companies failed to anticipate the growth of automobile and air transportation—and their own demise—because they defined themselves as being in the "railroad business," not transportation. The same process is at work with the Japanese. A company such as Toyota is keenly aware that it might be climbing a sinking mountain that could vanish from view, just as the railroads did. However, Toyota does not have much of an option—diversification efforts into non-auto industries (such as housing construction) have not been successful. Like Toyota, most Japanese companies keep doing what they have been doing since the end of World War II—even though their future might be clouded.

Exhibit 9:3 summarizes the strengths and weaknesses of Japanese myopia, a sobering list indeed. For each of the strong points, such as "keeps eye on the task," there is a corresponding weakness, such as "forgets the objective." As Kotler quips: "Having lost sight of our objective, we redoubled our effort."[141]

Exhibit 9:3
Strengths and Weaknesses of Myopia

Strengths	Weaknesses
Sees details clearly	Misses the big picture
Keeps eye on the task	Forgets the objective
Does not tire	Keeps going regardless of aim
Learns task very well	Learns only immediate task
Stays focused	Difficult to multitask
Forces strong task definition	Requires complete specification of task
Learns to do the job even better	Gets limited skills
Is reliable and predictable	Lacks imagination
Understands own job and the company's job	Has no independent perspective on self or company

One drawback of the Japanese focus on details is that it requires a very well-specified task, a positive when the path to the top is well-known and stable, but a drawback when the linkage is incompletely understood. We expect the Japanese to be adept at benchmarking, where the task is to identify precisely a competitor's strengths and weaknesses. Even targeting a leading brand is conceptually straightforward, although not necessarily technically easy.

Now that Japanese companies like Matsushita, Toyota, and Canon have achieved leadership status in global markets, the paths are no longer so clear. What should the new products be? Which technologies should we focus on? How should we pursue new strategic alliances? Many of the large Japanese corporations as yet lack the leadership necessary to blaze new trails. Their incapacity is a matter not of establishing new visions, because they can and have done so, but of associating the vision to feasible actions in their organizations, of spelling out the end-to-end chains, implementing their visions. The traditional reliance on bottom-up management and capable middle managers works better when the job at hand is clear, but has made top-down management much more difficult than for their Western counterparts with more rationally oriented training. Japanese management must give employees new tasks appropriate to the changed circumstances and new visions; otherwise the Japanese companies will simply repeat old routines in response to external pressures. The close-to-the-customer tradition and the clearly defined role of the marketer vis-à-vis the customer outlined in the previous chapters need to be wedded to stronger and more innovative leadership at the top. Execution, where the Japanese excel, needs to be guided by a new road map.[142]

REENGINEERING THROUGH TEAMS

These new road maps are as likely to come from middle management and front-line personnel as from top management. The Japanese companies attempt to engage all employees in the drive to chart new paths, develop new thinking, and, in fact, create new knowledge. The practices of the Japanese "knowledge-creating company" have been thoroughly documented by Nonaka and Takeuchi (1995). From a marketing perspective, the practices are interesting because they demonstrate how companies mobilize all employees to learn more about markets and how to captivate customers. And they help the company reengineer without laying off people. Instead of lowering costs, the practices are aimed at raising revenues.

A brief example from 7-Eleven shows what is involved. All employees of Ito-Yokado, the parent of 7-Eleven, hold weekly team meetings to share experiences and generate new ideas about more efficient deliveries, new products, merchandising, promotions, etc. The meetings are not simply a verbal and quick form of sharing specifics about explicit proposals, but also intended to allow the sharing of informal and tacit knowledge through socializing. Through these frequent meetings people get to know each other, ideas of what has worked in some stores can quickly be shared, contacts for assistance with implementation are made available, and so on. It is a team approach, and the spirit pervading the meetings is one of mutual support—without people feeling threatened about idea ownership, rewards—or layoffs.

The team approach is of course also now common in the West. But in the West it is assumed that when teams get together, the agenda should be clear, the roles well defined, and the progress measured. Such disciplined meetings are anathema to the Japanese, often to the chagrin of Western-educated employees who might feel that no significant progress is made. But the Japanese consensus-style, nonconfrontational, and sometimes irrelevant discussion has its own benefits. Since the focus among all employees is on the business anyway—the Zen way—there is less reason to fear veering off the path. Add to that the recent findings among social science researchers in the West that decision-making accuracy is, surprisingly, improved when teams are allowed to discuss issues not directly relevant to the task at hand.[143] Frequent meetings among small teams of all employees seems not only a good way to create new options and motivate people—it also might carve out the new "straight and narrow path."

The fundamental lesson is that rather than asking managers to set long-term objectives, we should guide their efforts to identify the linkage between such long-term goals and today's activities. If we know what we can do today for future benefits, both Westerners and Japanese alike will create forward-thinking strategy and work toward it in the moment.

INTUITION AND FOCUS

But of course there are useful lessons in the Japanese emphasis on intuition and focus. Successful Western companies have already adopted many of the Japanese marketing practices, and are attempting to adopt the underlying customer philosophy as well. Here are the five major lessons for the marketing manager.

• In every market, nurture grass-roots relationships with consumers and middlemen so that you can make or rely on intuitive judgment calls when necessary.

Blind intuition, without an understanding of the actual marketplace, can be misleading and dangerous. Among Western marketing professionals, who tend to move easily among industries, intuition from one market does not necessarily transfer and apply to new market contexts. For example, when John Sculley moved from Pepsi soft drinks to Apple computers, he could rely upon his experience with off-the-shelf products, but not with the new channels of distribution. Apple's problems, and Sculley's subsequent departure, revolved around Apple's attempts to strengthen its share of the business market, which required very different middlemen and the traditional IBM/DOS market's acceptance of new technology. Similarly, when launching Newton (the original hand-held personal assistant computer), Sculley was out of his depth, trying to intuit market acceptance of a new technology.[144]

• Balance or temper sophisticated techniques of market analysis with the underlying intuition about markets and customers.

Most market plans require hard data analysis of markets, when available, and a quantified prediction of product performance. But numbers are never enough. Harold Geneen's management style at the old conglomerate ITT, which relied on financial reports of specific business targets, was no longer tenable when global competition heated up, and Rand Aareskog decided to sell off units for which there was no in-depth business knowledge in ITT. Managers must understand how to motivate middlemen, how to talk to customers, and how to anticipate competitors. Many of these softer factors require intuitive judgments, informed by hands-on research, but also by a wide variety of other information sources. Redundancy increases information reliability, and even the best forecast requires managerial judgment about managerial capability and environmental factors. Mitsubishi's ill-fated purchase of Rockefeller Center and other trophy assets, the speculative developments of golf courses, and Sony's and Matsushita's forays into Hollywood and the banking missteps that underpinned this expansion show what happens when the Japanese ignore their own principles of intuitive incrementalism, as they did toward the end of the high-flying 1980s.

• When market uncertainty is high and predictions are difficult, take one step at a time, and make haste slowly.

Instead of developing a complete marketing plan for unknown or unpredictable markets, test market an existing product in one local area, monitor and learn from the market reaction, regroup, and try again. Any large commitment, of people, finances, or time requires a smart strategic plan unless you have no choice. But the grand plans are useless and, worse, induce inflexibility when forecasted scenarios are not realized. When Benetton, the Italian apparel maker, expanded rapidly into the U.S. market in the 1980s, it ended up with a large number of store owners who were not well-trained and a warehouse and distribution system that did not have sufficient capacity. It took the company a couple of years to regroup and shift to a gradual expansion, starting with the larger metropolitan areas.

With a trial-and-error strategy, you can gradually learn more about the market and limit your exposure. The strategy requires *flexibility*, because you must correct errors, and implement the learning in the next step. It also requires *speed* of execution, since your competitors will learn from your testing. Market timing becomes crucial. Wal-Mart entered Mexico when the peso was tied to the dollar and, perhaps learning from Benetton's problems, expanded gradually through a joint venture with Cifra, a local retailer. As Wal-Mart learned more about the market, it started opening its own stores in Mexico. Because of the gradualism, when the peso was devalued in early 1995, Wal-Mart could quickly reduce its exposure by limiting the expansion pace.

- Customers require product functionality and high quality—and much more!

Trumpeting one's unique selling propositions (USPs) in advertisements is passé. Your product features, even quality, do not remain unique for long. Although some Western advertisers, such as some U.S. auto firms, seem slow to recognize the shift (perhaps because they are steeped in "benefits" thinking), competition in many globalized markets has shifted to value-added status, image, and customer service. With targeting of competitive products, benchmarking against leading brands, and sharing of product platforms for me-too versions, value-added factors differentiate the brands. It can be difficult to be original in advertising when products are so similar and target the same segment. Despite using different agencies, in 1995 the Chevrolet Blazer and the Ford Explorer came out with almost identical TV commercials, a man fishing for trout in a mountain stream, with the vehicle in view on the side of the river. It is not surprising if commercials become increasingly weird—but for good business it is important to remember that knowledgeable dealers and good after-sales service create a lot of value added too.

- Forget the false notion that your company "owns a market" because of unique sustainable advantages.

Sustainable competitive advantages as given are dead in the water. In today's free and open markets, competitors with new products can shift customer preferences quickly. Technological advances are rapidly diffused, targeted leaders have trouble defending their brands against me-too-plus, and even non-Japanese companies must compete on time. The success of Snapple in the alternative beverage market took Coca Cola and Pepsi by surprise, and as they tried to regroup with Fruitopia and Lipton Originals, another small company introduced Arizona with great success. The solution is not only to sustain your advantage by destroying it and renewing it through new products, new technology, and new value-added features, but also to execute your renewal better than the competition. Renewal is a tough job, especially if your ego and past successes get in the way.

THE CHALLENGE FOR THE WEST

Western companies, like the Japanese, are steeped in culture. But where the Japanese managers still believe they work for the company and the society at large, their American counterparts find such allegiance misguided. Where Western employees try to maximize their choice in the labor market, Japanese managers and workers try to maximize the chances of their company surviving, and find themselves together visiting customers and stocking shelves in supermarkets. Where the shareholders of a Western company generate returns on investment by pressuring management, Japanese owners *help* manage the company. Such differences affect the ability of the company to change strategies and implementation.

THE NEED FOR EXECUTION

The biggest headache for a Western company in emulating the Japanese practices is execution. Sure, a company can broaden its vision and work with a longer time horizon by tying bonuses and executive compensation to long-term objectives, as the Campbell soup company and the Heinz company have done. It can aim for quality as Xerox did in the early 1980s. It can target the same market segments as the Japanese do. But the real problem lies in implementing the strategies. Western companies falter in execution.

The implementation phase of any strategic shift pits the Japanese culture squarely against the Western, East versus West. It relates to how people define their self-worth in the job and leave their egos at home, as in the Japanese workplace. Frontline employees are below their customers, not equals—but they keep their value as human beings. They provide service when the customer needs it, not when the seller can offer it. The relationships rest on common personal grounds and economic need—the economics being so obvious that they don't want to mention it. It is a community of sorts.

JUST DOING IT

The company that wants to adopt the best of the Japanese approach must take a long look at what it can realistically implement with its current resources of employee skills and know-how—including the degree to which productivity and efficiency are narrowly defined and measured short-term. The common case occurs when ability and willingness to adopt a customer-based and Japanese-style marketing philosophy both exist, but when incentives and control systems prohibit execution. As Deming says, the problem is not the people, but the system. It represents a reengineering in reverse, obliterating efficiency-oriented systems and installing effective alternatives.

The Japanese transplants in Europe and the Americas have proven it possible. The American auto plants of Toyota, Nissan, and Honda export quality cars back to the Japanese market, showing how U.S. workers can work as well as anybody. At dealerships where the employees are locals, such as Toyota's Camry and Honda's Accord and Civic, Americans sell and service American-made models with outstanding customer satisfaction scores. In England, comparisons of marketing execution between Japanese transplants and domestic firms show a consistent pattern of superiority for the transplants, comprised largely of British managers and workers.[145]

Thus, Western people can do it. True, the Japanese transplants have often been located in areas outside industrial cities like Detroit, in homogeneous and stable communities, in rural areas of Ohio, Kentucky, and Wales rather than around the traditional factory or union towns. Careful screening and testing of job applicants minimize the chance of hiring people fundamentally opposed to the "my company, my family" orientation. But while this may affect manufacturing, many dealers and retail stores offer more than one manufacturer's product line, and the hiring is usually done by the independent owner.

Training is one key in the success. Japanese managers consider training very important, and they are good teachers, not surprising when one remembers that the companies generally hire at entry levels only. They are not simply content with developing courses and training programs, and on-the-job training rotations. Following the *kaizen* principle of constant improvement, they also follow through. Although the process is at work throughout marketing and manufacturing, it appears most obviously in in-store service and customer satisfaction. To create satisfied customers, companies send managers and technicians to visit dealers, distributors, and stores, helping to instill a high level of attention to detail. Toyota's dealers in Australia, for example, watch a videotape in which a Toyota representative visits a local dealer to point out areas that need improvement: no chairs in the showroom, room temperature too high, old carpet, sloppy dress and approach to the customer by the salesperson, manner of speaking, and so on.[146] The details themselves are less striking for a Westerner than the Japanese touches. For example, the dealer is taught how to keep a list of things to check, greeting routines for the employees' customers to open and close the day, dress to wear and words not to use, names of customers and prospects to record and remember, and so on. The approach is akin to that of Disney's famous stylizing of its "cast members" in the theme parks. As at Euro-Disney in France, such a personality makeover is not universally accepted by native workers. But, as Toyota impresses on its Australian dealers, it works. And, as the American books on services attest to, such training is now common fare elsewhere also in the United States. Apart from training, however, managers must create incentives to induce the frontline people to execute the new strategies. Standard operating procedures (such as answering the telephone politely within three rings, always standing up when the customer enters, never speaking against a competitor's product) must become basic requirements for treating the customer well. Beyond that, managers must empower the line people to take initiatives that are not covered—such as taking care of the customer's dog, answering children's questions, and calling for a cab for the customer. In Western companies, such empowerment often runs counter to the productivity measures used to rate employee performance, and budget restrictions force employees to eliminate any "surprise and delight" to the basic service. The drive for efficiency, however well-intentioned, can ruin excellent service in Western companies, while Japanese companies, with a sense of "the customer comes first," are much more likely to keep executing well. A firm where managers and workers are reluctant to work selflessly for the company will struggle in adopting the new principles—or in competing with the Japanese.

A reliance on strong policy rather than analysis goes counter to what most scientifically oriented business schools in the West have taught for the last thirty years or so. Needless to say, the Japanese sometimes choose the wrong product to introduce or the wrong market to enter or the wrong partner to do business with. Simple analysis could often have predicted such an outcome, and although any Western firm's scientific evaluation of alternatives may not necessarily have a better track record, policy-based decisions often represent a damn-the-torpedoes strategy. The Japanese, however, know you must work to make even a good strategy pay off. Even less-than-optimal strategies can work—given enough time and effort. When you get married you don't set up a "payback" period after which you reevaluate the arrangement. You make it work. You execute.

NOTES

1. This example is described in detail by Urban & Star (1991, pp. 240–260).
2. The lack of specific position descriptions or marketing departments is well-documented; see, for example, Kagono (1984) and Clark (1979).
3. See, for example, Abegglen & Stalk (1985), Kagono et al. (1985), and Pascale & Athos (1981).
4. See Kagono (1984) and Pucik et al. (1989).
5. See Tokita (1990) and Tung (1993).
6. The importance of "even the littlest rock" was pointed out in the early Benedict (1946) work, and reemphasized in the Doi (1971) writings. The application to business organization can be found in, for example, Clark (1979), Cole (1979), and Sakiya (1982).
7. March (1990) discusses what Westerners have to do to overcome such a "natural" entry barrier to the Japanese market. Itami and Roehl (1987) show how these kinds of invisible assets can be built.
8. Representative references include Ozawa's (1994) *Blueprint* book, Tasker's (1992) book on the end of Japan's golden era, and articles by Fulford (1992) and Hirano (1994).
9. See Abegglen (1958).
10. Because of consumer protection laws in the United States, many of the negative consequences from the distrust are eliminated. There is less need for trust when the customers have the law on their side. At the same time it is important to recognize that some domestically oriented and protected Japanese industries have been less than candid in their dealings with customers. Housing and road construction, aluminum smelting, and insurance are some areas with a spotty record. The intensely competitive export-oriented Japanese companies are the focus here.
11. See, for example, Moore (1995); Gates (1995).
12. In the typical stock market analogy, an "arm's-length" market transaction means that the buyer is willing to buy and the seller is willing to sell, and only the price is negotiable. This misses the point that in the typical retail situation for products the price is not negotiated. After the seller sets prices, the buyer makes a decision whether to buy. The seller is not allowed to raise price for "undesirable" customers, for example. The stock market analogy can be extended by specifying a sufficiently long "repricing period" to allow price realignment—but the customer can then be lost to a competitor. In competitive product markets, the buyer has the upper hand.

13. These behaviors clearly reflect the cultural norm of avoiding conflict (cf. Hofstede 1984) and come less naturally to Western service employees (as discussed by Riddle 1988, and Schlesinger & Heskett 1991).

14. From the Japanese viewpoint, the "empowerment" movement in Western companies, by which employees are given increased responsibilities, attempts to harness the employees' need for ego gratification, and direct it toward company goals. For the Japanese employee, the only power available comes from the company, which "empowers" the employees by hiring them (for more about the human resource aspects of Japanese organizations, see Clark 1979, and Okimoto & Rohlen 1988).

15. The new personal service literature in the West now recognizes this. See, for example, Albrecht (1992).

16. This is also undergoing change in the West, propelled by the customer satisfaction drive for high quality and the subsequent positive impact on the motivation among company employees—see, for example, Fornell (1992).

17. Similar sentiments are now of course also voiced in the West, even though the predominance of functional product attributes is hard to avoid when products still don't perform—see, for example, Carlzon (1987); Albrecht (1992); and Schlossberg (1993).

18. These terms, although derived from the practices at the automobile companies, are also common in other Japanese industries. This is a result of the intense knowledge diffusion that takes place among Japanese companies.

19. Much of the material for these examples is from the Japanese-language book, *Sony's Quality Renaissance* (1992) and other case material (in Japanese) from the Japan Management Association, translated by Misako Litt.

20. Personal service in the West is gradually improving as competition between functionally comparable products shifts to intangibles, and the importance of service is recognized. The pressure for high productivity does, naturally, tend to go counter to some of these efforts, and require managerial fine-tuning. For example, in the Subway company, a franchised deli-style food service operation on the U.S. East Coast, sandwich servers are asked to handle twelve to fifteen customers per hour—and not to go beyond that, so as not to compromise service given.

21. See Asai (1987).

22. To the Japanese, and perhaps to Westerners as well, tipping involves an implicit measurement of another person's worth. For this reason, a too-small tip is sometimes angrily rejected by a Western taxi driver, for example. In contrast, the rejection of tipping in Japan is based more on a desire to avoid having the tipper lose face by miscalculating the provider's worth.

23. The system of *nakodo* (go-between) is well-developed in Japan. Teachers, doctors, and other professionals who may have natural access to potential customers are approached by company salespeople who ask them to be *nakodos* and recommend their products. The kickback commissions collected by the teachers are often an important part of their income and one reason that, for example, teaching positions at state universities, although with low nominal pay, are very attractive.

24. See Carlzon (1987).

25. It is perhaps only fair to note that, at least in the United States, any expression of sorrow is readily turned into a confession of guilt, with dangerous legal implications. The reluctance of service providers in the United States to say "Sorry" is perhaps something for which the litigious society can be blamed.

26. An excellent recent version is the accomplished volume by Urban & Star (1991), which uses quantitative analysis to attack case-based problems.

27. By the same token, it has been more difficult for the Japanese to figure out the different Europeans—as it probably is for the Europeans as well. And Japanese officials have been caught flatfooted several times by American trade negotiators such as Mickey Kantor, whose lawyer experience and savvy make him neither explicit nor transparent.

28. This is also why the Japanese are often accused of speaking with two voices.

29. As we will see later in the book, the preoccupation with the development of needs and wants goes well with the emphasis among Japanese companies on new product introduction and proliferation.

30. See Mintzberg (1994).

31. The Honda and Toyota approaches have been quite fully documented by "benchmarking" American competitors, including Chrysler and GM.

32. See, for example, Peppers and Rogers, 1993, and Hohisha, 1996.

33. The Japanese have tied such observations directly into product design, partly with the help of American professionals—see Konno (1991) and Norman (1990).

34. Representative sources include Sasaki (1990) and Konno (1991).

35. See, for example, Toyoda (1985) and Pascale (1984). For a vivid account of the managers behind Nissan's U.S. entry, see Halberstam (1986).

36. Based on personal interviews with Canon managers.

37. See, for example, Ohmae (1988).

38. See Hamel & Prahalad (1991).

39. See, for example, Deming (1986).

40. The negotiation literature bears witness to this—see, for example, Graham & Sano (1984).

41. A 1990 quote from Mitchell Reed, then president and CEO of Grey-Daiko in Tokyo.

42. This illustration is drawn from a personal interview with the general manager of the subsidiary.

43. This is not to say that the level of financial risk faced by Japanese investors is higher than that of their Western counterparts. Rather, what is reported is the perceived uncertainty often voiced by Japanese about political, economic, and social factors in Western markets.

44. From the *Washington Post*, April 12, 1995, p. 11.

45. The immersion in data and the resulting redundancy effects are basic to the "knowledge-creating" company—see Nonaka and Takeuchi (1995).

46. European penetration shows a more scattered pattern. Because of the fragmentation of the continent into different countries, Japanese companies have a less unified approach, and uneven presence across the countries.

47. See Johansson & Segerfeldt (1987).

48. It is interesting to note—but not surprising—that many of the examples

given in Stalk & Hout (1990) about the advantages of competing on time come from Japanese companies.

49. From Johansson & Segerfeldt (1987).

50. Representative examples include the books by Day (1984) and Aaker (1988) on strategic market management.

51. Pascale's 1984 account of Honda, and Toyoda's 1985 description of the Toyota problems both make for fascinating reading.

52. The book by Quinn (1980) is a classic statement of the principles of strategic incrementalism and shows that incrementalism is not confined to the Japanese.

53. This absence of cost-and-benefit analysis is similar to that described by Ghemawat (1991, chapter 2) for some principled Western companies in ethical cases.

54. Halberstam's (1986) discussion of Nissan's trials and tribulations is a vivid description of one company's entry strategy.

55. The large trading company Itohchu's promotion of Jay Chai, a Korean who speaks fluent Japanese, to be CEO of its New York office is still considered remarkable (*Washington Post* 1995).

56. Reported in Johansson & Segerfeldt (1987).

57. See Stalk & Hout (1990).

58. This should not hide the fact that the way to get to the technological front often involves working closely with lead customers—see von Hippel (1988).

59. The Newton debacle has been widely discussed in the media—see, for example, the *New York Times*, December 12, 1993 (Markoff 1993).

60. In marketing, the Bonoma (1985) treatment of strategy implementation should be recognized. Bonoma makes a valiant case for some principles of implementation.

61. See, for example, Johnson (1982).

62. From Lyons (1976, chapter 12). The Morita (1986) book on Sony and the Sakiya (1987) volume on Honda also offer good examples. So does the entertaining book on Nissan's American entry by Halberstam (1986), which offers a good example of intuitive incrementalism at work.

63. The Honda initiative is discussed by Sakiya (1982). Morita (1986) explains the Walkman case. The Toshiba introduction is based on personal interviews in Toshiba and is discussed in more detail in chapter 5.

64. See Ghemawat (1991).

65. *Wall Street Journal*, September 24, 1986.

66. See Ohmae (1988).

67. Figures provided by Tadao Kagono, Professor at Kobe University, in a 1994 interview.

68. The term "churning" was proposed in a 1990 speech by Kevin Jones, formerly of McKinsey, Tokyo, now at Booz-Allen & Hamilton, Hong Kong (Jones 1990).

69. See Moore (1995, chapter 4).

70. See Schnaars (1994).

71. Personal interview with Masumi Natsuzaka, Regional Sales Manager, Kao Corporation, Tokyo, July 15, 1994.

72. See Hamel & Prahalad (1994, chapter 10).
73. See Porter (1985, p. 217).
74. See Ohmae (1988).
75. See Hanssens & Johansson (1991) for an empirical demonstration of the synergy effect in the case of automobiles.
76. See Moore (1995, p. 90).
77. Saab's relatively small size also made it difficult to leverage its first-mover advantage—it has since been acquired by General Motors.
78. See Abegglen & Stalk (1985, chapter 3).
79. The information about Asahi Super Dry is drawn from "Asahi Breweries, Ltd." (Harvard Business School case no. 9–389–114) and from "Supersellers: Japan's Marketing Innovators," *Business Tokyo*, April 1988, pp. 8–12.
80. See Gates (1995).
81. The Toshiba laptop discussion is based on a personal interview with Mr. Hiroe on May 24, 1991.
82. The beachhead strategy is well-described by Kotler et al. (1985, chapter 5).
83. The unexpected market success of the Japanese luxury cars has been a topic of several news reports. See, for example, *New York Times Auto Supplement*, April 3, 1994, and *Business Week*, January 24, 1994.
84. A good expression for this spirit is found in Sasaki's work on the total quality movement, which deplores the weak execution among Western firms (Sasaki 1990).
85. Of course, using the same agency is not so strange in Japan where one agency can handle work for several direct competitors.
86. The parallelism is discussed at length in Abegglen & Stalk (1985).
87. LaBarre (1994).
88. See, for example, Papadopoulos et al. (1989).
89. The "visions" common among Japanese top executives (such as "Computers and Communications" from Koji Kobayashi at NEC or "Creative Life" by Suntory's Keizo Saji) signify both a unique mission and a common purpose (Kagono et al., 1985).
90. See Cooper (1994).
91. For an up-to-date discussion, see Czinkota & Kotabe (1993).
92. See Solomon (1994, p. 195). Nissan's soft-sell introduction for the Infiniti seems not to have prohibited the car from gaining market acceptance.
93. The Cheer example is drawn from a term project report by Masumi Natsuzaka, University of Washington, October 1985. With the recent recession and growth of discounting, the role of promotion in Japan is increasing (Johansson & Hirano, 1994).
94. See Sakakibara & Westney (1992).
95. See Sakakibara (1990).
96. See, among many contributions, Schonberger (1986), Takeuchi & Nonaka (1988), and Womack et al. (1990).
97. See Hauser & Clausing (1988).
98. See Johnson (1994).
99. For more detail on design for manufacturing, see, for example, Schonberger (1986). The *kaizen* concept is discussed well by Sasaki (1990).

100. This is an adapted version of a diagram first shown by Kevin Jones, formerly of McKinsey, Tokyo, now at Booz-Allen & Hamilton, Hong Kong.
101. See, in particular, Hamel & Prahalad (1991).
102. See Sakakibara & Aoshima (1989). With 1996 model introductions in the Acura line, Honda is pursuing more of a full-line strategy.
103. See Johansson & Hirano (1994).
104. These and other similar examples are reported by Prestowitz (1988).
105. For more on the well-known experience curve effect, see, for example, Stalk & Hout (1990, chapter 1).
106. See, for example, Wheelwright & Clark (1992), Cooper (1994).
107. A term used by Cooper (1994).
108. For more detail on knowledge creation in Japanese firms and several in-depth examples, see Nonaka & Takeuchi (1995).
109. The target pricing and costing techniques are given a fuller description in English in Cooper's excellent new case compendium (Cooper 1994).
110. As reported in the *New York Times*, October 13, 1992, D12.
111. The Makino quote is from a personal interview in Tokyo, December 21, 1986.
112. See Kelly (1982).
113. See Fields (1989).
114. The main source for the Nike discussion is the *Harvard Business Review* interview with Phil Knight, November-December 1990.
115. The brand name listings are from companies' annual reports and product catalogs. Ownership can shift over time, of course. Black & Decker, for example, is now independent of GE.
116. The agency business in Japan is dealt with in more detail by other writers. See, for example, Fields (1989), and the *Advertising Age* special issue on Japan, April 25, 1989.
117. See Carlzon (1987).
118. As in Halberstam's (1986) book, comparing Nissan and Ford.
119. See Toyoda (1985).
120. See, for example, the Alderson (1957) classic on executive action.
121. The Czinkota & Woronoff (1986) book deals with the many layers that contribute to the low productivity.
122. See Maruyama (1993).
123. The use of vending machines for the sale of beer is striking, since it means minors can buy alcohol relatively easily. But the Japanese society is sufficiently tight-knit that such abuses are rare. The owners of the liquor stores that stock the machines are responsible for keeping an eye on usage, and the local police box at the corner is usually not far away. But when foreign workers came to Japan at the end of the 1980s, some break-in problems were reported.
124. The Kao material is partly drawn from a report on Kao's marketing system by Noriko Miyajima, Takashi Izuhara, and Erik Newton, MBA students at the International University of Japan, June 14, 1991.
125. The club concept is not unique to Japanese companies—see, for example, Mary Kay cosmetics, catalog houses, and various store memberships—but

the Japanese application is perhaps both more extensive and more intensive.

126. The material here is drawn from Munns (1994).

127. The discussion of 7-Eleven draws on Munn's (1994) thesis.

128. Personal interview with Masumi Natsuzaka, Regional Sales Manager, Kao Corporation, Tokyo, July 15, 1994.

129. See, for example, Toyoda's (1955) and Halberstam's (1986) accounts for the auto industry.

130. Several of Honda's American managers accused of bribery pleaded guilty (see *New York Times*, February 8, 1996, D1, D5).

131. These casual comments are from personal interviews with the managers involved.

132. Personal interview with Tadao Kagono, Professor at Kobe University, July 14, 1994.

133. The Kotler et al. (1985) book offers a more structural explanation for the Japanese entry strategies. In retrospect, even a trial-and-error strategy can look methodical and systematic, very much the way the path to a new scientific discovery can be explained ex post facto. Conversely, even a structured approach needs to allow flexibility and sequential learning as new information flows in. The difference is the degree to which plans are specified before the first move.

134. See Levitt (1960).

135. A good presentation of the long-term view can be found in Abegglen & Stalk (1985, chapter 8).

136. A good summary of the quality movement can be found in Garvin (1988).

137. *Tatemae*, the public self, and *honne*, the private self, are common terms in Japanese descriptions of their own behavior. The terms are sometimes confusing to Westerners, who tend to take the *honne* as "real" and therefore expressive of the true intentions. The fact is, *tatemae* is a better predictor of Japanese behavior in a business context. Japanese businessmen do not do what they "want" to do, but what they have to do.

138. This example uses an image first developed in Pirsig (1974), and used very effectively to describe the striving for "quality."

139. See, for example, the recent Gallup survey reported by La Barre (1994).

140. See Levitt (1960).

141. From Kotler's fifth edition (1984, p. 743).

142. One is struck by the fact that as late as 1991, when protectionist pressures threatened the Japanese auto imports into the American market, Toyota employees dedicated themselves to a corporate goal of "renewed efforts to improve productivity" (see *Japan Times*, May 21, 1991).

143. See, for example, Weisband (1995) and Galegher et al. (1990).

144. See Cooper (1995). The Sega strategy was discussed in a front-page story in *Business Week*, February 21, 1994.

145. See Doyle et al. (1986).

146. From an interview with Mr. Shigeru Handa, CS Manager, Toyota Sales, Tokyo, January 14, 1992.

GLOSSARY

anime. Cartoon; animation.

hachimaki. Headbands worn during festivals.

happi coats. Short, kimonolike robes made of cotton and worn during festivals.

honne. The true thought and wishes of an individual. One is supposed to conceal one's *honne*. See *tatemae.*

kacho. Section chief; considered the first level in middle management. The general order of promotion is *kakaricho* (subsection chief); *kacho; bucho* (division chief).

kaizen. Improvement or reform; in this context, *kaizen* implies continuous improvement.

kamisama. A god; literally "honored deity."

karoshi. Death from overwork. This phenomenon has been documented extensively in Japan.

manga. Comic magazines. Japanese comic books cater to every segment of the population. Different *manga* are marketed to housewives, businessmen, teenagers, children, etc.

mikoshi. A portable shinto shrine, supported on a litter and displayed during festivals. Festival participants carry the *mikoshi* on their shoulders while walking.

nakodo. The matchmaker who arranges a marriage.

okyakusama. Guest; literally "honored guest." Used for customer.

sangen. Three actuals approach.

sashimi. Raw fish sliced into thin rectangular shapes.

tatemae. The outward facade one presents to society. See *honne.*

tenji kai. "Postmortem" meeting in connection with reverse engineering.

SELECTED REFERENCES

Aaker, David. *Strategic Market Management.* 2nd ed. New York: Wiley, 1988.

Abegglen, James C. *The Japanese Factory: Aspects of Its Social Organization,* Glencoe, IL: Free Press, 1958.

Abegglen, James C., and George Stalk Jr. *Kaisha: The Japanese Corporation.* New York: Basic Books, 1985.

Albrecht, Karl. *The Only Thing That Matters.* New York: HarperBusiness, 1992.

Alderson, Wroe. *Marketing Behavior and Executive Action: A Functionalist Approach to Marketing Theory.* Homewood, IL: Irwin, 1957.

Asai, Keizaburo. *The Production Strategy of Service.* Tokyo: Dobunkan, 1987 (in Japanese).

Bagozzi, Richard. "Marketing as Exchange." *Journal of Marketing,* April 1978: 231–44.

Benedict, Ruth. *The Chrysanthemum and the Sword.* Boston: Houghton Mifflin, 1946.

Bonoma, Thomas V. *The Marketing Edge: Making Strategies Work.* New York: The Free Press, 1985.

Carlzon, Jan. *Moments of Truth.* Cambridge, MA: Ballinger, 1987.

Clark, Rodney C. *The Japanese Company.* New Haven: Yale University Press, 1979.

Cole, R. E. *Work, Mobility and Participation.* Berkeley: University of California Press, 1979.

Cooper, Robin. *Cost Management in a Confrontation Strategy: Lessons from Japan.* Cambridge, MA: Harvard Business School, 1994.

Cooper, Robin. *When Lean Enterprises Collide: Competing through Confrontation.* Boston: Harvard Business School Press, 1995.

Czinkota, Michael R., and Jon Woronoff. *Japan's Market: The Distribution System.* New York: Praeger, 1986.

Czinkota, Michael R., and Masaaki Kotabe. *The Japanese Distribution System.* Chicago; Cambridge, England: Probus, 1993.

Day, George S. *Strategic Market Planning.* St. Paul, MN: West, 1984.

Deming, W. Edwards. *Out of the Crisis.* Cambridge, MA: MIT Center for Advanced Engineering Studies, 1986.

Doi, Takeo. *The Anatomy of Dependence.* Tokyo: Kodansha International, 1971.

Doyle, Peter; John Saunders; and V. Wong. "A Comparative Investigation of

Japanese Marketing Strategies in the British Market." *Journal of International Business Studies.* Spring 1986: 27–46.

Fornell, Claes. "A National Customer Satisfaction Barometer: The Swedish Experience." *Journal of Marketing,* vol. 56, no. 1 (January 1992): 6–21.

Fulford, Benjamin. "After the Boom." *Business Tokyo,* January 1992: 18–21.

Galegher, Jolene; Robert Kraut; and Carmen Edigo, eds. *Intellectual Teamwork: Social and Technological Foundations of Cooperative Work.* Hillsdale, NJ: L. Erlbaum Associates, 1990.

Garvin, David A. *Managing Quality.* New York: Free Press, 1988

Gates, Bill. *The Road Ahead.* New York: Viking, 1995.

Ghemawat, Pankaj. *Commitment: The Dynamic of Strategy.* New York: Free Press, 1991

Graham, John L., and Yoshihiro Sano. *Smart Bargaining: Doing Business with the Japanese.* Cambridge, MA: Ballinger, 1984.

Halberstam, D. *The Reckoning.* New York: Morrow, 1986.

Hamel, Gary, and C. K. Prahalad. "Corporate Imagination and Expeditionary Marketing." *Harvard Business Review,* July–August 1991: 81–92.

Hamel, Gary, and C. K. Prahalad. *Competing for the Future.* Boston: Harvard Business School Press, 1994.

Hanssens, D. M., and J. K. Johansson. "Rivalry as Synergy? The Japanese Automobile Companies' Export Expansion." *Journal of International Business Studies,* vol. 22, no.3 (1991): 503–26.

Hauser, John R., and Don Clausing. "The House of Quality." *Harvard Business Review* 66 (1988): 63–73.

Hirano, Masaaki. "Performance of Foreign Firms in Japan: Is Japanese Management Any Good?" Working Paper, Institute for Systems Science, Waseda University, Tokyo: 1994.

Hofstede, Geert. *Culture's Consequences.* Beverly Hills, CA: Sage Publications, 1984.

Holusha, John. "Making the Shoe Fit, Perfectly." *New York Times,* March 20, 1996: D1, D7.

Itami, Hiroyuki, with Thomas W. Roehl. *Mobilizing Invisible Assets.* Cambridge, MA: Harvard University Press, 1987.

Johansson, Johny K., and Jan U. Segerfeldt. "Keeping in Touch: Information Gathering by Japanese and Swedish Subsidiaries in the U.S." Paper presented at the Academy of International Business Meeting in Chicago, October 1987.

Johansson, Johny K., and Masaaki Hirano. "Japanese Marketing in the Post-Bubble Era." *International Executive,* Jan/Feb 1996: 33–51.

Johnson, Chalmers. *MITI and the Japanese Miracle.* Stanford, CA: Stanford University Press, 1982.

Jones, Kevin. Presentation at the YPO (Young President's Organization) International Conference in Nagoya, Japan, 1990.

Kagono, Tadao. *How Japanese Companies Work.* Osaka: Kansei Productivity Center, 1984

Kagono, Tadao; Ikujiro Nonaka; Kiyonori Sakakibara; and Akihiro Okumura. *Strategic vs Evolutionary Management.* Amsterdam: North-Holland, 1985.

Kawasaki, Guy. *How to Drive Your Competition Crazy*. New York: Hyperion, 1995.

Kelly, Dan. "Where Mood Speaks Louder Than Words." *Advertising Age*, August 23, 1982: M2–M3.

Konno, Noboru. *The Logic of Design*. Tokyo: Kodansha, 1991 (in Japanese).

Kotler, Philip. *Marketing Management*, 5th ed. Englewood Cliffs, NJ: Prentice Hall, 1984.

Kotler, P.; L. Fahey; and S. Jatusripitak. *The New Competition: What Theory Z Didn't Tell You About Marketing*. Englewood Cliffs, NJ: Prentice Hall, 1985.

LaBarre, Polly. "Quality's Silent Partner." *Industry Week*, vol. 8, no. 243 (April 18, 1994): 47–8.

Levitt, Theodore. "Marketing Myopia." *Harvard Business Review*, July–August, 1960: 45–56.

Lyons, Nick. *The Sony Vision*. New York: Crown, 1976.

March, Robert M. *The Honourable Customer*. Melbourne: Longman Professional, 1990

Markoff, John. "Marketer's Dream, Engineer's Nightmare." *New York Times*, December 12, 1993: Section 3, pp. 1, 8.

Maruyama, Masayoshi. "The Structure and Performance of the Japanese Distribution System." In: Czinkota, Michael R., and Masaaki Kotabe. *The Japanese Distribution System*. Chicago; Cambridge, England: Probus, 1993.

McCarthy, E. Jerome. *Basic Marketing*. Homewood, IL: Irwin, 1960.

Mintzberg, Henry. *The Rise and Fall of Strategic Planning*. New York: Free Press, 1994.

Moore, Geoffrey A. *Inside the Tornado: Marketing Strategies from Silicon Valley's Cutting Edge*. New York: HarperBusiness, 1995.

Morita, Akio. *Made in Japan*. New York: NAL Penguin, 1986.

Munns, Peter J. S. *Marketing and Distribution in Japan Today*. Master's thesis, Graduate School of Management, International University of Japan, 1994.

Nonaka, Ikujiro, and Hirotaka Takeuchi. *The Knowledge-Creating Company: How Japanese Companies Create the Dynamics of Innovation*. New York: Oxford University Press, 1995.

Norman, Donald. *The Design of Everyday Things*. New York: Doubleday Currency, 1990.

Ohmae, K. "Getting Back to Strategy." *Harvard Business Review* 66 (1988): 149–56.

Okimoto, Daniel I., and Thomas P. Rohlen, eds. *Inside the Japanese System*. Stanford, CA: Stanford University Press, 1988.

Ozawa, Ichiro. *Blueprint for a New Japan*. New York: Kodansha, 1994.

Papadopoulos, N.; L. A. Heslop; and G. Bamossy. "International Competitiveness of American and Japanese Products." In: N. Papadopoulos, ed. *Dimensions of International Business No. 2*. Ottawa, Canada: International Business Study Group, Carleton University, 1989.

Pascale, Richard T. "Perspectives on Strategy: The Real Story Behind Honda's Success." *California Management Review*, vol. 26, no.3 (Spring 1984): 47–72.

Pascale, Richard T., and A. G. Athos. *The Art of Japanese Management*. New York: Simon and Schuster, 1981.

Peppers, Don, and Martha Rogers. *The One to One Future*. New York: Doubleday, 1993.

Pirsig, Robert. *Zen and the Art of Motorcycle Maintenance*. New York: Bantam Books, 1974.

Porter, Michael E. *Competitive Advantage*. New York: Free Press, 1985.

Prestowitz, Clyde V. Jr. *Trading Places: How We Allowed Japan to Take the Lead*. New York: Basic Books, 1988.

Pucik, V.; M. Hanada; and G. Fifield. *Management Culture and the Effectiveness of Local Executives in Japanese-owned U.S. Corporations*. Ann Arbor: University of Michigan, 1989.

Quinn, James Brian. *Strategies for Change—Logical Incrementalism*. Homewood, IL: Irwin, 1980.

Riddle, Dorothy I. "Culturally Determined Aspects of Service Quality." Paper presented at the Quality in Services Symposium, University of Karlstad, Sweden, September 1988.

Sakakibara, Kiyonori. "Meaningful Space of a Product." Working paper, Hitotsubashi University, Kunitachi, Tokyo, 1990.

Sakakibara, Kiyonori, and Yaichi Aoshima. "Company Growth and the 'Wholeness' of Product Strategy." Working paper, Graduate School of Commerce, Hitotsubashi University, 1989.

Sakakibara, Kiyonori, and D. Eleanor Westney. "Japan's Management of Global Innovation: Technology Management Crossing Borders." In: Nathan Rosenberg, Ralph Landau, and David C. Mowery, eds. *Technology and the Wealth of Nations*. Stanford, CA: Stanford University Press, 1992: 327–43.

Sakiya, Tetsuo. *Honda Motor: The Men, the Management, and the Machines*. Tokyo: Kodansha, 1987.

Sasaki, Naoto. *Management and Industrial Structure in Japan*, 2nd ed. New York: Pergamon Press, 1990.

Schlesinger, Leonard A., and James L. Heskett. "The Service-Driven Service Company." *Harvard Business Review*, September–October 1991: 71–81.

Schlossberg, Howard. "Dawning of the Era of Emotion." *Marketing News*. Chicago: American Marketing Association, February 15, 1993: 1–2.

Schnaars, Steven P. *Managing Imitation Strategies*. New York: Free Press, 1994.

Schonberger, Richard J. *World Class Manufacturing*. New York: Free Press, 1986.

Solomon, Michael R. *Consumer Behavior*, 2nd ed. Needham Heights, MA: Allyn and Bacon, 1994.

Sony Quality Renaissance. Tokyo: Japan Management Association, 1992 (in Japanese).

Stalk, George Jr., and Thomas M. Hout. *Competing Against Time: How Time-based Competition is Reshaping Global Markets*. New York: The Free Press, 1990.

Takeuchi, Hirotaka, and Ikujiro Nonaka. "The New New Product Development Game." *Harvard Business Review*, January–February 1986: 137–46.

Tasker, Peter. *The End of the Japanese Golden Era?* Tokyo: Kodansha, 1992.

Tokita, M. "Internationalization of Corporation and Management Philosophy."

Consensus Management 4 (1990): 4–9

Toyoda, Eiji. *Toyota: Fifty Years in Motion.* Tokyo: Kodansha, 1985.

Treacy, Michael, and Fred Wiersema. *The Discipline of Market Leaders: Choose Your Customers, Narrow Your Focus, Dominate Your Market.* Reading, MA: Addison-Wesley, 1995.

Tung, Rosalie E. "Managing Cross-National and Intra-National Diversity." *Human Resource Management,* vol. 32, no. 4 (Winter 1993): 461–77.

Urban, Glen L., and Steven H. Star. *Advanced Marketing Strategy: Phenomena, Analysis, Decisions.* Englewood Cliffs, NJ: Prentice Hall, 1991.

von Hippel, Eric. *The Sources of Innovation.* New York: Oxford University Press, 1988.

Weisband, Suzanne. "Assessing Divergent and Convergent Processes in Face-to-Face and Computer Mediated Groups." Working paper, Department of MIS, University of Arizona, Tucson, October 1995.

Wheelwright, Stephen C., and Kim B. Clark. *Revolutionizing Product Development.* New York: Free Press, 1992.

Womack, James P., Daniel T. Jones, and Daniel Roos. *The Machine that Changed the World.* New York: Rawson Associates, 1990.

INDEX

Quality function deployment (QFD), 109–10, 113
Questionnaires, 38, 44
Railroad industry, 17, 162
Ralph Lauren, 127
RCA Corporation, 82, 116, 132, 139
Reebok International, Ltd., 4, 138
Reengineering, 12, 13, 34–5
Research and development, 107, 119
Retailers
    advertising and, 137–8, 141
    manufacturers and, 143, 147, 149, 153
    supermarkets, 148
    See also Salespeople
Retail sales, 171n. 12
Reverse engineering, 87, 94, 103, 109, 111–3
Revlon, Inc., 122
Richardson-Vicks, Inc., 139
Ricoh Company, Ltd., 157
Rise and Fall of Strategic Planning (Mintzberg), xvii, 40
Ritz-Carlton Hotel Company, 4
Rockefeller Center (New York), 64, 166

Saab Scania A.B., 63, 86, 88, 175n. 87
Sailor Moon, 69–70
Sakakibara, Kiyonori, 124, 154
Salespeople, 172n. 23
    and customer complaints, 32–4
    as employees, 20, 22
    information gathering by, 56
    prepurchase information from, 10, 18–9, 137
    relations with customers, 10, 18–9, 20–1, 22
Sam's Club, xvi
Sangen principle, 41, 55, 110, 118
Sanrio Company, Ltd., 70, 116
Sanyo Electric Company, Ltd., 139–40

Sapporo Breweries, Ltd., 89–90, 136, 138
Sashimi process, 108, 120
Saturn Corporation, 15, 16, 34
Scandinavian Airlines System, 4
Schnaars, Steven, xvi
Schulhof, Michael, xiii, 140
"Science" of marketing, 6, 7, 36
Sculley, John, 165
Seagram Company, Ltd., 140
Sega Enterprises, Ltd., 44, 69, 98
Seiko Instruments, Inc., 85, 92
Service, after-sales, 10, 25–7, 154, 157
Service, personal, 29–32, 172n. 20
7-Eleven Japan Company, Ltd., 48, 152–3, 155, 164
Shareholders, 12, 159, 168
Sharp Corporation, 50, 81, 87, 88
    organizational reforms, 120–2
Shinkansen bullet trains, 17
Shiseido Company, Ltd.
    consumer clubs, 150
    and distribution, 143, 148, 149, 150
    and market research, 117
    and retail discount sellers, 151–2
    and U.S. market, 62, 64, 107, 151, 155
Silicon Valley, 81
Situational ethics, 38
Sloan, Alfred P., Jr., 70, 124
Snapple Beverage Corporation, xiv, 167
Social status, 8
Software industry, 15–6
Sony Corporation, xiii, 130, 140
    Betamax VCR development, 73–4, 82
    and cannibalization, 83–4
    and churning, 82, 83–4
    competition with Matsushita, 73, 82, 88
    and corporate identity, 140